Recovering Spirituality is a remarkable book. Ingrid Mathieu uncovers aspects of spirituality and recovery that clarify many of the struggles addicts—both clean and not so clean—deal with. Her insights into spiritual bypass, its dangers and potential, will inform my own teaching and recovery. If you are in recovery and wondering why you feel stalled, or if you are working with someone who is struggling with the program, read this book. It will open doors you didn't even know were there.

—KEVIN GRIFFIN,
AUTHOR OF *ONE BREATH AT A TIME: BUDDHISM
AND THE TWELVE STEPS, AND A BURNING
DHARMA GOD & THE PA*

Recovering Spirituality is a rich in recovery who (knowingly o. ...u for a spiritual escape from the difl .....stead, Ingrid Mathieu offers an authentic, spi. path of living in the here and now and of being present to this wonderful, precious life. Don't miss this book.

—TÉRÈSE JACOBS-STEWART,
AUTHOR OF *MINDFULNESS AND THE 12 STEPS*

With great compassion and wisdom, Dr. Mathieu points out how walking the spiritual path in general, and specifically as a tool of recovery from addiction in any form, is a very subtle process with sidetracks, bypasses, and self-deceptions into which aspirants may fall, challenges that are common within all spiritual practices. *Recovering Spirituality* is a powerful, loving guide to spiritual maturity, psychological self-reliance, and emotional clarity. I highly recommend it.

—MICHAEL BERNARD BECKWITH,
AUTHOR OF *SPIRITUAL LIBERATION:
FULFILLING YOUR SOUL'S POTENTIAL*

A very important, lucid contribution to recovery literature, clearly exposing the very real problems that spiritual bypassing (the use of spiritual beliefs and practices to avoid dealing with pain and unresolved issues) poses in organizations like AA. For anyone involved in any way with AA, this is a book that should be carefully read and taken to heart.

—ROBERT AUGUSTUS MASTERS, PHD,
AUTHOR OF *SPIRITUAL BYPASSING: WHEN SPIRITUALITY
DISCONNECTS US FROM WHAT REALLY MATTERS*
AND *MEETING THE DRAGON: ENDING OUR
SUFFERING BY ENTERING OUR PAIN*

This much-needed and deeply important book offers profound insight into the human mind and heart. It looks deeply into the practice of spiritual bypassing—the use of spiritual ideas and practices to attempt to sidestep one's own unfinished emotional business. To my knowledge, *Recovering Spirituality* is also the first book to apply such inquiry to the process of recovery from addiction. In unraveling some of the mysteries of relapse and stalled recovery, it also offers an entirely unexpected twist on spiritual bypassing itself. A very valuable book for anyone in recovery—and anyone with a spiritual practice.

—SCOTT EDELSTEIN,
AUTHOR OF *SEX AND THE SPIRITUAL TEACHER*

RECOVERING
SPIRITUALITY

RECOVERING SPIRITUALITY

Achieving
Emotional Sobriety
in Your Spiritual Practice

Ingrid Mathieu, PhD

Hazelden
Publishing

Hazelden Publishing
Center City, Minnesota 55012
hazelden.org/bookstore

ISBN: 978-1-61649-089-8

Library of Congress Cataloging-in-Publication Data

Mathieu, Ingrid, 1974-
    Recovering spirituality : achieving emotional sobriety in your spiritual
practice / by Ingrid Mathieu.
        p. cm.
    Includes bibliographical references (p. 179).
    ISBN 978-1-61649-089-8 (softcover)
    1. Recovering addicts--Religious life. 2. Addicts--Religious life.
3. Twelve-step programs--Religious aspects. 4. Spirituality. I. Title.
    BL625.9.R43M38 2011
    204'.42--dc23
                            2011016721

Editor's note: The names, details, and circumstances have been changed to protect the privacy of those mentioned in this publication.

Alcoholics Anonymous, AA, and the Big Book are registered trademarks of Alcoholics Anonymous World Service Inc.

The brief excerpts from *Alcoholics Anonymous, Twelve Steps and Twelve Traditions, 'Pass It On,' A.A. Comes of Age* and from the pamphlet *Questions & Answers on Sponsorship* are reprinted with permission of Alcoholics Anonymous World Services, Inc. (AAWS). Permission to reprint these excerpts does not mean that AAWS has reviewed or approved the contents of this publication, or that AAWS necessarily agrees with the views expressed herein. A.A. is a program of recovery from alcoholism *only*—use of these excerpts in connection with programs and activities which are patterned after A.A., but which address other problems, or in any other non A.A. context, does not imply otherwise.

Direct quotations from *Textbook of Transpersonal Psychiatry and Psychology,* copyright © Bruce W. Scotton, Allan B. Chinen, John R. Battista, are reprinted by permission of Basic Books, a member of the Perseus Books Group.

Brief quotes from pages xii, 5, 134, 150, 182, and 200 from *Stages of Faith: The Psychology of Human Development and the Quest for Meaning* by James W. Fowler are copyright © 1981 by James W. Fowler. Reprinted by permission of HarperCollins Publishers.

"Wild Geese" from *Dream Work* by Mary Oliver. Copyright © 1986 by Mary Oliver. Used by permission of Grove/Atlantic Inc.

Cover design by David Spohn
Interior design and production by David Farr, ImageSmythe
Copyediting and production management by Jean Cook, ImageSmythe

Dedication

THIS BOOK IS DEDICATED to Claire Wineland, one of the wisest and kindest spirits I have been fortunate to know and love. They say that it takes a village to raise a child—but this child has truly raised a village. Thank you Claire, for all you have taught me about courage, compassion, gratitude, and grace. Thank you for sharing your creativity and your friendship. I am a better person because I know you.

Contents

Acknowledgments   xi

Introduction   1

PART ONE

CHAPTER ONE   14
Allison

CHAPTER TWO   28
What Is Spiritual Bypass?

CHAPTER THREE   42
Bill's Story Revisited

CHAPTER FOUR   54
Spiritual Bypass and Twelve Step Recovery

CHAPTER FIVE   66
Bradford

CHAPTER SIX   80
The Softer Side of Spiritual Bypass

CHAPTER SEVEN   94
Chelsea

PART TWO

CHAPTER EIGHT   110
There Is No Finish Line

CHAPTER NINE   118
Lost in Translation

CHAPTER TEN   126
In My Defense

CHAPTER ELEVEN   136
My Way or the Highway

CHAPTER TWELVE   148
Becoming Right Size

CHAPTER THIRTEEN   158
Integration Leads to Integrity

IN CONCLUSION   164
Putting It All Together

EPILOGUE   172
The Hoop Is Wider Than You Think

Bibliography   179

About the Author   185

Acknowledgments

I AM SO GRATEFUL TO THE AA MEMBERS who participated in the research for this book. They willingly provided their time, their trust, and the opportunity for me to witness true courage, humility, and honesty. Without their articulate, personal reflections, this endeavor would have been impossible.

Throughout this journey, many individuals have provided their expertise and support. I am forever indebted to the following people for helping to make this dream a reality. Thank you to Beverly Berg, John Creswell, Katie Cusick, Ron Diliberto, Rachel Drews, Jay Edwards, Sid Farrar, Loretta Grant, Vivien Kooper, Gisela Kunstler, David Laramie, Martin Mathieu, Hillary Metz, Suzanne Oaks-Brownstein, Peter Schletty, Jennifer Schmidt, Bob Schmitt, and Marvin Seppala.

Introduction

MANY PEOPLE ARE ATTRACTED to the practices of positive affirmations, vision boards, and other tools of manifestation because of the cash and prizes they are promised if they follow a simple routine. Who doesn't want to believe we can procure all of our heart's desires? Who doesn't want to take the fast track to contentment and serenity? Although there is nothing wrong with these aspirations, or with the various ways we aim to achieve them, practices that are only grounded in abundance and tranquility tend to abandon the seeker when scarcity or emotional turmoil are present. Although incredibly seductive, anything that promises the light without acknowledging the shadow isn't telling the whole story.

We are fallible human beings. We can easily get caught up in the notion that God is a bank teller or an orchestrator of our heart's every desire. We want to believe that spirituality will propel us not only toward enlightenment but toward riches and everlasting emotional bliss. We don't want to walk through the tough stuff in life, so we gravitate toward the book, program, or path that promises to show us how to avoid it. But "it" doesn't go away so easily. Everybody experiences pain, and we don't always get exactly what we want. Even the spiritual path that doesn't deny our suffering can be used with the intention of navigating around hardship. I believe this is just part of being human. We are drawn to the light just like a flower to the sun. However, unless we stay rooted, plugged into the dirt, we won't be able to survive.

We might use the realities of life to tell ourselves that we must not be "doing it right" or that something is wrong with us because we don't feel "happy, joyous, and free" all the time. Or we may feel judged by others for having a difficult emotional experience amid all the tools and tricks that could free us from such discomfort. And thus, the cycle begins. We search for the next quick fix. Yesterday's yoga class is today's vegan diet. We swap chanting for meditation and try visiting a new church. We increase our commitment to altruism and find a new healer, psychic, or trainer. We decide that reading literature is out and putting pen to paper is in.

If you understand this cycle, and may even be able to add a few more "fixes" to the list, you might be longing for a spiritual path that you can follow in all conditions—material and otherwise. Perhaps you're longing for spirituality that doesn't run you ragged looking for perfection and that brings you comfort in whatever circumstance you may find yourself. I believe that many of us are truly yearning for a spiritual path that allows us to be whole human beings—with faults and assets, troubles and triumphs—because the truth is that we will never transcend the human condition, and we need a spirituality that can cope with *that* reality.

It turns out there is a concept that captures the phenomenon I've described. It is called *spiritual bypass*. Spiritual bypass is a defense mechanism by which we use spiritual practices or beliefs to avoid our emotional wounds, unwanted thoughts or impulses, or threats to our self-esteem. A simple example of this defense is when we believe that if we pray hard enough, or in the right manner, we can escape our painful feelings. We are experiencing spiritual bypass when we expect our spiritual practices to "fix" our problems, rather than to be with us in the midst of them.

When I realized there was language for this experience, I could not stop thinking about it. I was both curious about and dumbfounded by the fact that so many of us have been trying to walk a spiritual path—whatever that means to each of us, whether religious or not religious—only to get tangled up in the illusion that spirituality is a method for controlling obstacles and outcomes. We were earnestly and openly doing our spiritual work without realizing that the ways in which we were using the tools were actually in service of perpetuating our shortcomings. Consciously, we wanted to evolve. Unconsciously, we wanted to stay comfortable and in control.

John Welwood coined the term *spiritual bypass* in an article for *The Journal of Transpersonal Psychology* titled "Principles of Inner Work: Psychological and Spiritual," and many others have touched on the subject over the years. This is the first book entirely dedicated to the topic. My intention is to extend the preliminary conversations on spiritual bypass in such a way that a new vernacular arises. My hope is to raise awareness about spiritual bypass, so that individuals might identify the defense in their own lives. I want to reveal the many forms of spiritual bypass, so it becomes less theoretical and more identifiable. I want people to have permission to be spiritual beings while having a human experience. I am not trying to put down or pathologize spiritual practice; I am attempting to bring more consciousness to spiritual practice as it relates to one's psychological nature.

Living in a culture that perpetually advertises the next quick fix, I have personally experienced spiritual bypass many times. Drifting toward the defense not only guarded me against my feelings, but it allowed me to strive for my goals in a way that was "spiritual"—which, let's face it, didn't look so bad on the outside. As an action-oriented person who loved the idea that someday I could "get it right," I pursued spirituality, psychotherapy, yoga, education, ad infinitum, in the hope that I would reach a finish line of sorts. I longed to feel *good* with the expectation that I could overcome the *bad*, primarily my feelings of worry and shame. In my life, the notion of "arriving" has been a rather appealing one.

Although my various pursuits of betterment have been rewarding, my investigation of spiritual bypass has allowed me to see the naïve beliefs that I had about spiritual practice and the human condition. I've since learned that I cannot bypass my feelings, my history, or the essence of who I am. Trying to overcome such things only pushed the proverbial finish line even farther away. No matter what I did, what I achieved, or what I understood about myself—at the end of the day I was, and am, still *me*. Thus, my striving for enlightenment and clarity, embedded in the goal of surpassing myself, only made my feelings of worthlessness grow.

I have finally redefined my personal finish line from "becoming someone" to accepting who I am and where I am in my life. I can retain a sense of purpose and intention; the difference is that I try not to use my spiritual path as an escape hatch for the present. Instead of discovering a golden road, free of frailty and emotional turmoil, I am learning to love those parts of myself that I once rejected. This newfound "love and tolerance" was not the starting point for this book. The research I conducted on spiritual bypass was rooted in my desire to "get it right" and the defense mechanism seemed all wrong. I have been truly surprised at where this investigation has taken me during the last five years. Even as I write these words, my understanding of mind, body, and spirit is ever-evolving. The minute I think, "I get it," I'm actually just beginning another stage of awareness. Investigating consciousness is funny that way— we don't know what we don't know.

What I can say at this point is that spiritual development is not a black-and-white endeavor in which you are either evolving or you're not. And spiritual bypass is just another way we defend ourselves from the painful realities in life. Sometimes we need a little defending, and other times we need to shed our defenses to find more freedom. Although spiritual bypass may not be ideal, neither is the human condition. Understanding the nature of spiritual bypass has allowed me to soften toward myself as a perpetually imperfect person and toward others for being in the same boat.

But getting back to where it all started, my personal experience of spiritual bypass led to many questions that I was hoping to answer: If I was unintentionally using spirituality to avoid hurt and pain or to control a particular outcome, was it really detrimental? How does spiritual bypass affect people? Is there such a thing as an unhealthy spiritual practice? And if so, what separates it from a healthy practice? Is spiritual bypass harmful? And if it is, what are the repercussions? If not, how might it be serving people in some way? I was eager to answer these questions, as I did not want to fall into the trap of thinking that I was a bad person—or that my spirituality was deficient—because it did not manifest all that I was longing for. Nor did I want to collude with my psychotherapy clients who had such convictions.

I did want to find out how the pieces of the puzzle could fit in such a way that we are allowed to be both spiritual and sentient. I wanted to investigate the sort of magical thinking that had us believing we could rise above the difficulties our earthly peers were experiencing. I wanted to see if there was a way to amplify the blind spots in our spiritual practices, so that we might strive toward greater acceptance of our humanity, rather than unconsciously sliding into our psychological frailties, all the while retaining the benefits that spiritual practice and belief can offer.

Having worked extensively with recovering alcoholics, a population of people well known for attempting to avoid their feelings (or humanness), I saw many examples of spiritual bypass in people recovering from their addictions. Because Alcoholics Anonymous (known as AA or "the program") is a spiritual program designed to help alcoholics stay sober, a defense mechanism that employs spirituality as a protector from emotional distress appeared to be a likely one for AA members.

Addicts tend to be sensitive individuals with mind-sets that gravitate toward symptom relief. This characteristic does not disappear when someone enters Twelve Step recovery, which makes it very likely that, at some point, the recovering person will use the program just as he used his drug of choice. Instead of drinking to fend off feelings, the alcoholic will pour himself into service or Step work, hoping that these actions will quell his emotional turmoil as sufficiently as the alcohol once did. He will use spiritual tools with the expectation that they will divert unwanted frustrations now that drinking is no longer an option. The alcoholic who tried every strategy to drink like a normal person will likely employ every imaginable spiritual solution to permanently defend himself against the fears that imprison him. He might need to guard against such things for a time to stay sober. If he were faced with the Truth (with a capital T) all at once, it would surely drive him back to the bottle. Thus, second-stage recovery, when one continually confronts underlying issues and feelings long after abstinence from drugs or alcohol has been established, is the reason so many people in recovery continue to go to meetings well into double-digit sobriety. Recovery is a process, fraught with a lifetime of growing pains, and certainly not for the faint of heart.

In addition to working a spiritual program and having a tendency to avoid painful feelings, recovering addicts are vulnerable to spiritual bypass because it is an unconscious occurrence. Just as we don't know when we are in denial until we have moved through it, so it is with spiritual bypass. It is not intended or consciously motivated. It is operating when we think we are actually walking an unadulterated spiritual path—talk about cunning and baffling! Spiritual bypass is sneaky that way. It is not as loud or visible as drugs or alcohol, but it can serve a similar purpose: to wrap the individual in a second skin of sorts, a protective barrier from the more daunting elements of our existence. We know that many people in recovery switch addictions when they get sober. A person will stop drinking and start compulsive overeating, for example. This phenomenon occurs because the person continues to need a mechanism that shields her from her existential dilemma. Spiritual bypass happens in much the same way, but rather than switching to another addiction, the person applies spiritual tools or principles "alcoholically." The *ism* in alcoholism colors the way in which the person thinks and acts with regard to her program.

As I learned more about spiritual bypass and began speaking with people in recovery about the defense, I was met with incredible enthusiasm. Almost everyone with long-term sobriety could identify a time when he had experienced spiritual bypass or he could recognize the defense in others. Recovering individuals were eager to talk about their experiences and they wanted to understand them better. They wanted to grow spiritually, not defensively, and some were concerned that spiritual bypass could lead to relapse. This collective interest led me to conduct my doctoral research on the experience of spiritual bypass by recovering alcoholics in AA.

In addition to working with many individuals in recovery, I've written the material in this book based on the study I conducted. The questions I had at the beginning of my inquiry have led to a clearer understanding of the pervasive nature of spiritual bypass and to candid reflections on how recovering addicts have moved through the defense in their own lives. It was revelatory to see how coming out of spiritual bypass could provide someone with more self-acceptance and compassion, with greater consciousness about what she is doing and why she is doing it, with freedom from the fears that propelled her toward bypass in the first place. Understanding spirituality as a defense has enhanced ongoing recovery, culminated in richer spiritual experience and profound appreciation for the human condition.

It is important to note that I use the terms *alcoholic* and *addict* in a general way throughout this book to mean all people in recovery in any Twelve Step program. If you are a debtor, gambler, alcoholic, drug addict, compulsive overeater or undereater, adult child of an alcoholic, sex and love addict, a member of Al-Anon, or a *human being*—this book is for you. It will address the subtleties of spiritual bypass by sharing stories of people in recovery. It will use the language of recovery wherever possible, and it will provide suggestions that encourage an integration of all human attributes in the context of working a spiritual program.

For anyone who fears that this book might be a criticism of the very program that saved your life, rest assured. I am not passing judgment on Twelve Step programs. From the moment that I learned of spiritual bypass, I have felt a deep calling to understand and clarify its effects for individuals in recovery. My hope is that Twelve Step programs will remain tethered to their divinely inspired roots while continuing to evolve with their members.

This book is an offering and, as such, is done in the spirit of the Twelve Step programs' tenet "Take what you like and leave the rest" that allows you to make decisions about what you will adopt into your recovery. Only you can know what constitutes spiritual bypass in your life, and only you can discern when it has been helpful or harmful. Just as the addict is the only person who can diagnose her disease of addiction, I am providing these theories and stories so that you might identify where and how spiritual bypass has operated in your life. In this way, spiritual bypass is a useful vehicle for looking at emotional sobriety and second-stage recovery, as it focuses on how people have felt stuck and how they have come to expand the fruits of their long-term recovery.

Part one of this book will share personal stories of spiritual bypass by members of AA. It will also define *spiritual bypass* and put it in the context of Twelve Step recovery. Part two will outline the themes that I arrived at by analyzing my research participants' experiences with spiritual bypass. These themes are grounded in spiritual and psychological theories and with relevant examples from my clinical experience working with addicts in recovery. This holistic overview provides something of a road map for spiritual bypass: what it looks like when you are in it, what you can do to move through it, and the benefits and challenges you might encounter along the way. I hope that it might provide some insight and direction to you in your ongoing recovery.

Terminology

Before we begin with our first story, it is important to define some terms and ideas that will be consistently presented throughout this book.

Spiritual Bypass

As a quick point of reference, spiritual bypass is a defense mechanism. Defense mechanisms are unconscious, psychological strategies that we all use to protect ourselves from emotional distress, threats to our self-esteem, and unwanted thoughts or experiences. Most of us are familiar with the defense mechanism of denial, when we refuse to acknowledge an issue in our lives. The defense mechanism of spiritual bypass protects us from underlying feelings by covering over or suppressing them via spiritual beliefs or practices. The purpose of this book is to thoroughly explore and describe spiritual bypass in the context of Twelve Step recovery.

Spirituality, Spirit, and Spiritual Practice

You can consider these terms as placeholders for your own definitions of such constructs. Although this list is certainly not exhaustive, some examples of definitions for spirituality include these:

- one's religious beliefs and practices
- belief in God or a Higher Power
- connection to oneself or others
- the experience of love

- trust in something Greater
- metaphysics
- relationship to nature
- mysticism
- faith of all kinds

Alcoholics Anonymous is a spiritual program that encourages members to choose a personal conception of a Higher Power. This inclusive way of thinking will also be used in this book, and I will use terms such as *Higher Power, God, Spirit,* and similar terms interchangeably.

As AA is a spiritual program, the tools and practices that a person employs while working the program can be considered spiritual in nature. This means that even if the person using the tools regards himself to be an atheist (someone who does not believe in God) or an agnostic (someone who doesn't know or believes that it is impossible to know whether God exists), he can still have an experience of spiritual bypass. For example, in this book you will notice that a person's process of working the Twelve Steps is associated with his experience of spiritual bypass. Although the person working the Steps might be an atheist, he can still use the program in a manner that bypasses his underlying feelings, which constitutes spiritual bypass (using a spiritual practice to avoid the human condition). In other words, people who consider themselves atheist or agnostic can still identify with the contents of this book, despite the word *spiritual,* just as they have found recovery in AA despite it being defined as a spiritual program.

Surrender

Rather than the classic idea of raising the white flag in defeat, surrender in the context of this topic is based on the Twelve Step idea of letting go. This includes releasing expectations and accepting things as they are, letting go of the illusion of control, making a decision to turn one's will and life over to a Higher Power, and becoming open to new ideas and possibilities—with or without a formal construct of God. As noted, an atheist or agnostic is just as capable of surrender as a recovering person who has a defined notion of a Higher Power.

Adaptive and Maladaptive

All defense mechanisms have adaptive and maladaptive attributes. *Adaptive* simply means flexible. We all experience adaptive defenses that help us to navigate the world. An example of an adaptive defense might be when we use humor to overcome an anxiety-provoking situation. We might laugh when we are terrified or tell a joke when we feel insecure. In general, defense mechanisms are adaptive until they lead to behaviors that threaten our emotional or physical well-being. When this occurs, they become *maladaptive*. Maladaptive defenses are likely involved when behavior is rigid and inflexible. If humor becomes the only tool for managing anxiety, one may have a difficult time in relationships or in fully functioning in life.

Although we will not use the terms *adaptive* and *maladaptive* a great deal, the concepts are important to understand. You may read in this book examples of spiritual bypass that appear to be maladaptive, but your own experience with the same practice has been adaptive—in other words, it hasn't hindered your overall progress in recovery. This is because actions or ideas themselves do not define something as adaptive (harmless) or maladaptive (harmful). The underlying drive and the outcome of the action determine its function. For example, prayer in and of itself is not a defense mechanism. When you pray as a way of avoiding uncomfortable feelings or the truth of your reality, however, prayer serves as spiritual bypass. If prayer carries you through a painful time to a place where you are better able to cope, this is an adaptive form of spiritual bypass. If prayer keeps you unconscious about your reality and leads to detrimental circumstances, this is a maladaptive form of spiritual bypass.

I want to be clear that there is no right or wrong way to engage in spiritual practice, and there is no concrete measuring stick for knowing when someone is, or is not, experiencing spiritual bypass. We each have only a personal experience of what works and what doesn't. This book illustrates some of the ways that others have been hindered and helped throughout their journeys. It is an exploration of the subtle nuances between adaptive and maladaptive defenses in Twelve Step recovery. I suggest that you let this material wash over you rather than that you interpret it as a set of instructions to follow. The specific stories and research findings are not static for all people at all times. Use this information as a jumping-off place for you to investigate what your own personal, subjective experience has been regarding spiritual bypass, whether it has been helpful or harmful, and how you hope to proceed in the future. This is the true work of second-stage recovery: to carve out a personal path on which to walk long after abstinence from your drug of choice has been established.

PART ONE

ONE

Allison

"Prayer and love are learned in the hour when prayer has become impossible and your heart has turned to stone."

— THOMAS MERTON

WHAT FOLLOWS ARE THE HIGHLIGHTS from an interview I conducted with Allison. The interview was designed to capture her personal experience of spiritual bypass in recovery. At the time of our discussion, Allison was fifty-three years old and had been sober for ten years.

Allison was a fashion designer in New York City when she got sober. Prior to recovery, her life seemed to be shrinking, and she was feeling increasingly more hopeless and miserable. She was leading a double life. During the day, she would dress up and project a sense of self-confidence. At night, she would rush home to blot out her existence with wine and marijuana. Although harder drugs were a part of her story, alcohol and pot were her drugs of choice.

Seven years before she came into AA, Allison flipped her car three times on the highway and she received her first DUI. Her arrest didn't do much to curtail her drinking or drug use. "You know, they make you go to some classes, but there was never any information about the program, no information about spirituality, the Steps, or any of that," she said. "And I completed that, because that is how you get your license back." Although Allison didn't get sober after this experience, she did make a promise to never drink and drive again. She was able to keep that promise; however, it was a given that she could be in a car with someone else who had been drinking, as long as she didn't get behind the wheel.

Years later, Allison's doctor admitted her to what Allison called a "scary rehab":

IT'S WHERE YOU GO IN AND THEY PUT YOU on medication, where it was mostly people off the street who were homeless and stuff like that—because he thought it would scare me. I remember my first day walking in and the patients thought I was a new nurse just because I looked good and I dressed well. They were shocked when I told them I was a patient. I was given medication and pretty much stayed in my room for a week. I remember thinking that when I got out I still had some pot at home, so I was planning not to drink, but I was gonna smoke. I left that place looking and feeling worse than when I went in. I took a taxi home, and I started smoking pot.

Allison would smoke marijuana every evening and every morning before she went to work. Her rationalization was "If you had to take the train every day, you would be smoking pot too." The smoking led to trying some "controlled drinking." During this time, she recalled the typical experience of buying an expensive bottle of wine when she got off the train from work, getting home, and immediately popping the cork. Before she took her first sip, she knew it wasn't going to be enough. Because of her promise not to drink and drive, she would have to go back to the same liquor store to buy more alcohol. The shame was so thick, she would profess to the store clerk, "Oh, we are having some guests over [at the] last minute, so I have to get more wine."

Eventually, enough was enough. Allison will never forget getting on her knees and asking God for help. She feels as though things started to change from that moment on. Although she didn't immediately stop drinking, she did drunkenly write a fax in really big letters to her doctor that read "Please help me. I need to get into rehab." She eventually entered a respectable treatment center, and when she arrived, she felt like she was home.

After three weeks in a rehab that introduced her to the concept of alcoholism as a disease that could be arrested one day at a time, Allison was dedicated to sobriety. She went home and attended ninety AA meetings in ninety days. She recalls early sobriety as a rebirth of sorts:

> GOING HOME AT NIGHT, I just stopped everything, you know, really protecting myself, putting myself in this womb. When I got home after a meeting, I would go to bed and eat popcorn and licorice and read my book. And my husband said to me, you know, "What is this—movie night every night?" And I just felt that I had to do whatever I had to do to protect my sobriety. I just knew that I couldn't go back. So I didn't go anywhere, and I was still smoking cigarettes (it took me a while to get off of that), and I knew that was okay, you know, as long as I wasn't smoking pot, or taking drugs, or drinking.

Allison's fear of relapse gave her the willingness to do anything to maintain her sobriety. She got on her knees every morning and every evening to thank God for another day sober. She began the process of recovery with an unquestioning faith in God and in the program.

> MY ENTIRE LIFE I HAD BEEN LOOKING FOR PEACE of mind and serenity. (I didn't know it was the word *serenity*, but that's what I was looking for.) And coming in to AA, I have always felt that God led me to AA and AA led me to God. So I have never had an issue with spirituality or my Higher Power, whom I choose to call God. I feel really grateful, you know,

because I have heard so many people struggling with those things. And I don't know where it came from, but I didn't question anything at all in the Steps. Everything was like, "This is it. Yeah, I'm gonna do this. I believe in this." I had no issues with any of it.

Allison's faith began when she was very young; she still owns a glow-in-the-dark cross from her childhood bedroom that reads "Trust God." It now hangs in her home and she laughed when she mentioned that "it still glows in the dark." On the whole, Allison's spiritual development in the program has been cyclical, rather then linear, in that she has encountered the same issues and spiritual concepts many times over. She began fervently reading spiritual books in early sobriety, starting with *Conversations with God*, books 1, 2, and 3. She also read books by the Dalai Lama and several others on creative visualization. She was trying to understand God and the Universe in a different way, to comprehend the nature of energy and the belief that we are all connected—that there is only One. At ten years of sobriety, Allison's literary pursuits included *The Artist's Way* and *The Science of Getting Rich*. The focus was on her creativity, the law of attraction, manifesting a bigger life, and abundance for all.

Her eclectic spiritual path has ultimately deepened her relationship to her Higher Power. Throughout her journey, Allison came to recognize various experiences of feeling as though she had surrendered to God, as well as times when she felt like she was intentionally holding on to self-will. In hindsight, she can also identify times where she unconsciously used spiritual tools or principles to remain in self-will, in spiritual bypass.

One example of spiritual bypass can be seen in her initial practice of the Twelve Steps. Admitting powerlessness in Step One was not a difficult task for Allison, and her belief in a loving God made Step Two fairly accessible. However, her early conceptions of God were rooted in projections of human attributes, which made it difficult for her to "turn things over" as Step Three suggests. For example, she saw God as a parent who punishes or rewards a child based on how she behaves. If Allison wanted to be rewarded, she had to be a good girl with good behavior. If she wanted God to forgive her for her wrongdoings, she needed to bestow that same level of forgiveness in her own life. Such rigid standards are not often realistic. They can strain people's ability to truly connect with their highest good or their Higher Power, primarily because they are asking themselves to disown so much of their true nature. It is like trying to connect with the Divine by disconnecting from yourself.

Allison also projected human attributes onto her Higher Power through her definition of unconditional love. In her experience, love was synonymous with material gain. Consequently, her belief in a loving God included the idea that He would give her what she wanted. This interpretation created the expectation that all of Allison's wants and needs would be provided for. Although she never investigated where this belief system came from, she mentioned that her self-centered stance as an alcoholic and her lack of humility probably had something to do with it. Additionally, Allison referred to the "pink cloud" of her early sobriety—a term that AA members use when everything in recovery feels "rosy"—as coloring her perception.

Allison's ideas about God in early sobriety led to some magical thinking about the Third Step. "I thought that Step Three was asking God for something, turning it over and not expecting it, and then getting it." She felt she deserved rewards for not drinking, above and beyond the reward of staying sober. As an example, she decided she wanted a diamond ring from her husband. In addition to wanting the jewelry, Allison was longing to feel worthy, accepted, and loved.

I REMEMBER GETTING ON MY KNEES and I said to myself, the old me would have asked him for it and been on him to get it, and I know I could have. But the new me thought, I'm not going to say a thing. I'm going to take . . . I didn't know it was contrary action . . . but I was gonna get down on my knees and pray to God.

Contrary action is based on the AA tenet that recovering addicts should behave in ways that are contrary to their natural desires. For instance, an addict who is craving drugs or alcohol would call her sponsor rather than directly giving in to the craving. In Allison's case of wanting a diamond ring, contrary action meant getting down on her knees and praying for God's will instead of pestering her husband for the gift. The action of not pestering her husband was clearly contrary to her natural desire and, up to this point, Allison was on track with the principle of Step Three, turning it over. However, her prayer was like a spiritual experiment, in which she went to God to get the ring instead of going directly to her husband. When her husband later returned with the gift, Allison's response was "Score! This Third Step stuff really works!" Although her actions *appeared* spiritual, she was attempting to spiritually manipulate the outcome of receiving the ring, which was not "turning it over" as Step Three suggests.

This experience with the diamond ring served as confirmation to Allison that God would provide exactly what she wanted if she took the right spiritual actions. Despite her sponsor stating that this was not an accurate description of the Third Step, this experience solidified her theory: take contrary action, and what you wish for will be provided.

A persuasive pull toward this belief system is that it allows you to maintain a feeling of control by believing you can influence your Higher Power. For Allison, this constitutes one example of spiritual bypass in her recovery, in that she used prayer and the posture of getting down on her knees to avoid feeling that she was unworthy or unlovable. Additionally, she sought to avoid potential feelings of disappointment, abandonment, and powerlessness.

This relationship to spiritual practice and to God initially felt fun and rewarding for Allison. However, during our interview, she explored how a God who rewards behavior might also have a downside. For example, she experienced a deep depression when she was nine years sober. Prior to the depression,

Allison had stopped her daily practice of getting down on her knees to pray. She remained in contact with her Higher Power, but her knees hurt too much to be kneeling on the floor. As she reflected on this experience, she began to wonder if her depression was caused by her change in spiritual practice. She felt as though a connection could be drawn between her decline in spiritual reverence and the depth of her emotional pain. This idea, although still rooted in Allison's perceived ability to influence God in a particular direction, began to shed light on how this conception of a Higher Power might not be of maximum benefit.

Another way Allison thought her thinking might have worsened her depression was through her beliefs about negative thinking. She was reading a lot of material about manifesting abundance and believed that she should have been controlling her thoughts in order to control her feelings. She believed that her attraction to negativity was causing her to spiral down in despair.

> **I HIT A REALLY DEEP DEPRESSION** and I wasn't turning it over. I was holding on to it. I was going to meetings, working with my sponsor, even reading this stuff—knowing that I can control my thoughts, that I can decide whether I am having negative thoughts or positive thoughts. I was picking the negative and I was going down. I was just going down the hole.

Allison shared about this experience in AA meetings, stating that she wished she could stop thinking altogether because of the power of her thoughts. She was trying to find some compassion for herself, but she feared that her depression would perpetuate the negative thinking and that the negative thinking would perpetuate the depression.

Over time, Allison became even more terrified and felt as though her "head was blowing up." Reading spiritual literature increased the feeling that she was doing something wrong because she felt so depressed. But when she pulled back on the reading and her daily practice of prayer, she felt she wasn't doing enough to stop the depression. "I literally felt like I was jumping out of my skin with this fear," she said, "and it was the first time that I really had a hard time turning things over." Allison was in much pain and felt completely powerless to change the way she was feeling. Her notions of being able to influence her Higher Power were not helping to relieve the depression, and she didn't know what else to do.

During this time, other people with long-term sobriety shared with Allison that she seemed to be beating herself up and that all she had to do was thank God for another day of sobriety. The old-timers' messages started to give her permission to be exactly where she was. She started to believe that it was okay to be feeling everything she was feeling. She didn't need to burden herself with the responsibility of influencing God or the course of her depression. These things were out of her control. And the truth was that despite feeling more pain than she had in her entire life, Allison wasn't drinking or using. This was the evidence that God was working in her life. Although she wasn't receiving the specific signs she was looking for, she was still being taken care of. Although the relationship looked different than it had in early sobriety, Allison was still maintaining a connection with God. When she recognized this, she started a new relationship with her Higher Power—and with herself.

When Allison looks back on her experience with spiritual bypass—magical thinking that she could control her Higher Power and her own experiences in life—she recognizes that it initially served as protection. If she believed God was handling all of the details in her life to her ultimate satisfaction, it was safe for her to let go of the drinking and drug use that had previously assisted her in defending against powerful emotions. The bypass created a cocoon, or a shelter, where it became possible to slowly release twenty-eight years of deep-seated ideas and habits. Knowing that you have to change *everything* in sobriety is a tall order, and she did her best to let go of what no longer served her while holding on to some comfort that her early perception of her Higher Power provided.

For Allison, the key to moving through spiritual bypass was to release the illusion that she could control or influence God, while simultaneously gaining more humility. The basic idea of humility in AA is to relinquish self-centeredness and to pursue the greater good. Allison advanced in her pursuit of humility when she hit a new bottom in her recovery. The phrase "hitting bottom" signifies the moment when an alcoholic has sunk low enough in his addiction to surrender to something greater than himself. In *Twelve Steps and Twelve Traditions*, Step One states "We perceive that only through utter defeat are we able to take our first steps toward liberation and strength."

Allison's depression, coupled with her fear and powerlessness over money and material success, ultimately led to her attending another Twelve Step program, Debtors Anonymous (DA). She acknowledged her substantial loss of income, her sizable spending habits, and the rather large debt she had amassed. She could no longer afford her lifestyle and started to see that her overspending and vagueness about money were really representative of her inability to take an honest look at herself. Becoming a newcomer in another program provided an opportunity to accept her powerlessness on a grander scale, to create a new conception of her Higher Power, and to strengthen her relationship to it.

I LITERALLY HAD TO HIT ANOTHER BOTTOM to get to a new surrender, and this change has been very humbling. I had an easier time accepting being an alcoholic than I did being a debtor. That has brought me much more shame—much, much more. But it is really the first time that I'm asking for help. I've been able to reach out to a new sponsor and to tell her what was really going on. And I'm a very private person. I'm very careful about what I say about myself in meetings, even my women's meetings. I'll let some things out, but I keep a lot of stuff close to the vest.

As Allison accessed this deeper relationship with God and with others in her new program, she recognized that she hadn't been taking advantage of one of the tools in AA—the act of *pausing* before she took impulsive actions. In AA's Big Book, it states,

> **AS WE GO THROUGH THE DAY WE PAUSE,** when agitated or doubtful, and ask for the right thought or action. We constantly remind ourselves we are no longer running the show, humbly saying to ourselves many times each day "Thy will be done."

The pause contained in "turning it over" was a crucial element in positively changing Allison's behavior. This aspect of Step Three included contrary action without the intention to control the outcome. Allison initially defended against her feelings through spiritual bypass to maintain sobriety, but she eventually learned to shed the defense so she could progress in her spiritual and psychological development.

Allison reconnected with the true meaning of surrender in this process. She recognized her shortcomings and was grateful for the chance to revisit spiritual ideas with fresh eyes. She became clear about her tendency to use action as a way of anesthetizing her feelings, and she sought to align herself with the ideal contained in *pausing*, knowing that she would never be perfect in this endeavor. She saw that ongoing recovery for her was a process of continually getting in touch with more reality.

Another component to moving through spiritual bypass for Allison was accepting that the way out of her depression was to go through it. She stayed with her feelings without attempting to change them or judging herself for having them. By participating in AA, she had learned from her peers that feelings are transient and temporal, not everlasting. With this in mind, she was able to endure her depression, while trusting that it would eventually shift. It was through accepting her painful experience with depression that Allison could reframe her conception of God from rewarding or punishing to a Higher Power that can be with her in all circumstances. This is another example of spiritual bypass as a beneficial aspect of Allison's recovery at one stage—obtaining sobriety through her belief that her Higher Power would relieve her of emotional difficulty—while eventually having to let go of the defense to cope with her present circumstances and move forward in her recovery. These experiences have enabled Allison to expand her relationship with God and to appreciate "life on life's terms," a phrase commonly used in AA to describe the idea that a sober life is not a perfect life, but one that is as human as the next.

Allison's current intention is to enlarge her connection with God in times of stress, as well as prosperity, by humbly listening for direction in her prayer and meditation. In addition, she appreciates the important part that action plays in working a spiritual program. She believes spiritual practice should not be an isolated endeavor and must be coupled with mental and physical development—typified in the AA adage "Faith without works is dead." Of course, the action must be tempered with acceptance for whatever is happening in the moment. Allison knows that she can't work her way out of her feelings or pray herself into exclusively receiving cash and prizes.

Allison's ability to see and describe her spiritual bypass arrived out of her self-awareness and from having some distance from the experiences. However, when her own story was reflected back to her toward the end of our interview, she only had partial recognition that bypass had occurred. Spiritual bypass is often an unconscious defense that some, like Allison, might want to hold on to in areas where it supports the illusion of control, while simultaneously letting go in ways that it restrains.

THE THING THAT BAFFLES ME RIGHT NOW is that I know this spiritual connection with God works, because every time I apply it, it does. So, why don't I use it more often? Why, as human beings, do we slip out of it? I wonder if that is the only way you can have growth and get more connected to God? Is it by getting away from God, seeing how that feels, and then having to go back? Because that is why I get so mad at myself, you know. I beat myself up about that. And my sponsor keeps reminding me, "You are only human. It is 'Progress, not perfection.'" But I get mad because I think I already know this, so why aren't I doing it? Or why do I subject myself to this kind of pain when I already know what the solution is? So, I think that would be my biggest question: why do I do that? And hearing from other people, why do we all do that? And then, who are the people like these monks, or like the Dalai Lama or whoever—do they have it down pat?

It is interesting to note that, just as the interview was ending in a place of trust and acceptance, Allison cycled back to the topic of desiring spiritual tools or ideas that might alter her experience for the better. She retains the belief that she is subjecting herself to pain, rather than accepting that pain is just another part of life. Although she knows some of her greatest spiritual experiences were born out of painful ones, she expresses self-judgment for her fallibility and still wishes to control and transcend it in some way. She is seeking evidence of such transcendence, and thus the cycle continues.

TWO

What Is Spiritual Bypass?

"Life itself flows from springs both clear and muddy."

— CARL JUNG

THIS QUOTE BY JUNG ILLUSTRATES the all-encompassing nature of life, ranging from tremendous joy to deep sorrow. When we favor one end of the spectrum over the other, we lose the appreciation for, and experience of, the whole. As spiritual bypass conceals the more painful experiences of life, the very nature of the defense is not a sustainable one. It is as though we are on a teeter-totter stuck in the up position—eventually we either land with both feet on the ground or we slide blisteringly to the other side. This sentiment is reflected in the saying "What we resist, persists."

To broaden our understanding of spiritual bypass, it is important to highlight some of the ideas that define and illustrate the defense. I will admit that this subject can be rather academic, with subtleties that are difficult to digest. However, it is important to bring this depth to our discussion, because spiritual bypass often occurs when we oversimplify spiritual concepts. We need to investigate the entire territory of spiritual bypass before we can draw a map that aids in easier travels. I have aimed to clarify pertinent material in this book without diminishing its relevance; however, those of you who wish for an even more thorough review of these topics might want to read any of the authors referenced throughout this book (see bibliography, page 179).

Given that John Welwood is the psychotherapist and spiritual practitioner who originated the term *spiritual bypassing,* let's begin with his reflections on the subject. In his book *Toward a Psychology of Awakening,* Welwood defined *spiritual bypassing* as "using spiritual ideas and practices to sidestep personal, emotional 'un-finished business,' to shore up a shaky sense of self, or to belittle basic needs, feelings, and developmental tasks, all in the name of enlightenment." He noted that spirituality includes experiences in the higher realms of human nature and that some people try to rise above basic human development by reaching these realms. In his experience, this tendency is particularly appealing for individuals who resist the more problematic or mundane aspects of life. In such cases, he has witnessed a propensity to create a new "spiritual" identity, which "is actually an old dysfunctional identity—based on avoidance of unresolved psychological issues."

To further this idea, Jack Kornfield encourages individuals on a spiritual path to face the full gamut of life's blessings and challenges. Kornfield is a clinical psychologist who was also trained as a Buddhist monk. In *Paths Beyond Ego,* he wrote that, "spiritual practice can easily be used to suppress and avoid feeling or to escape from difficult areas of our lives." He reminds people who are on a spiritual journey of the value in becoming more conscious in every aspect of life. Additionally, he believes that psychotherapy can aid a person in addressing critical facets of himself that are not attended to in prayer and meditation alone. Kornfield suggests people ask themselves, "Where am I awake, and what am I avoiding? Do I use my practice to hide? In what areas am I conscious, and where am I fearful, caught, or unfree?" These are excellent questions a person might ask as he investigates his relationship to spiritual bypass.

Charles Whitfield is a physician and expert on addiction and recovery who has written about the pitfalls of spiritual bypass. In the foreword to *Spiritual Awakenings,* he encourages all individuals in recovery to attend to their psychological wounding by reminding them of the following:

> We cannot let go of something if we do not know experientially of what we are letting go; we cannot transcend the unhealed; and we cannot connect experientially to the God of our understanding until we know our True Self, our heart.

These three authors have touched on the subject of spiritual bypass and believe it is an inherent challenge in bridging spiritual and psychological healing. Although their contributions have been tremendously important, what has been specifically written on the topic remains limited. Many other authors have written on subjects either closely related to spiritual bypass or seemingly derivatives of the defense. What follows is a review of such topics, beginning with *true* and *false spirituality.*

False Spirituality

Psychiatrist John R. Battista has written about the difference between healthy, or *true,* spirituality and unhealthy, or *false,* spirituality. In the *Textbook of Transpersonal Psychiatry and Psychology,* he distinguishes the two as "spiritual practices and beliefs that further the development and transformation of personality, and spiritual practices and beliefs that have been incorporated into a psychopathological personality." The latter category of false spirituality might also be identified as spiritual bypass. There are two types of false spirituality: defensive and offensive.

Defensive Spirituality

Defensive spirituality is the use of spiritual practices or beliefs to keep one from fully expressing herself. Battista cites the example of a Hindu, Buddhist, or Christian individual who rejects her anger, because such an expression opposes the precepts of her religion. "Spiritual defenses provide a rationale to disavow parts of one's self." Battista believes that rejecting aspects of one's self will serve to prolong suffering rather than transform it.

Spiritual defensiveness also occurs when a person blindly submits to an authority while rationalizing doing so as humility. In this form of the defense, she can avoid taking personal responsibility for her own life. One of the most tragic illustrations of this type of spiritual defensiveness occurred in 1978 when Jim Jones convinced his followers to partake in a mass suicide by drinking a grape-flavored beverage laced with cyanide and sedatives. Of course, milder versions of the defense might include the death of one's individuality, of personal goals and aspirations, or of the development of one's unique gifts.

Another instance of spiritual defensiveness is when a person is afraid to receive friendship or nurturance and rationalizes that fear as "God is the only source I need." This same idea can be extended to one's sexual wants and needs, when avoidance is rationalized as ascetic practice. Although there are certainly cases in which vows of chastity are admirable, when taken from a defensive stance they may be more congruent with one's fears than with one's faith.

Lastly, it is a spiritual defense when one fails to address biological and psychological problems such as depression, rationalizing these as "all of life is a spiritual teaching." Such a view ignores the fact that our existence is an embodied one. When we look at the definition of spiritual bypass, we can see that the defensiveness portrayed in all of these examples is at the core of the phenomenon.

Offensive Spirituality

Now let's look at the offensive form of false spirituality. Battista states that "offensive spirituality may be considered the narcissistic use of a spiritual persona or spiritual identification." Examples of this type of false spirituality are the guru who sexually exploits his followers or the spiritual seeker who uses a "higher consciousness scorecard," measuring one's frequency of prayer and meditation or one's spiritual development against that of another. Inherent in offensive spirituality is a feeling of superiority that Battista says "insists that others live up to a spiritual standard as a condition for a relationship while using the standard to avoid emotional conflicts and problems." A person who is engaged in offensive spirituality temporarily escapes her vulnerability by feeling as though she has risen above it.

Both defensive and offensive sides of false spirituality can be methods for avoiding the totality of human experience, and they highlight several forms of spiritual bypass. Another vehicle for spiritual bypass is *spiritual materialism.*

Show Me the Money

Chögyam Trungpa was the Tibetan meditation master who wrote *Cutting Through Spiritual Materialism*. He defined *spiritual materialism* as "deceiv[ing] ourselves into thinking we are developing spiritually when instead we are strengthening our egocentricity through spiritual techniques." Spiritual materialism occurs when someone aligns himself with a particular philosophy or spiritual group with the belief that doing so will relieve his suffering. A person might also believe that acquiring certain spiritual accomplishments or possessions will free him from pain or distress. Recall that John Welwood speaks of spiritual materialism as one aspect of spiritual bypass, because it is an unconscious attempt to use spiritual awareness as a solution for life's difficulties. In response to this tendency, Trungpa advises people on a spiritual path to "give up wishful thinking and accept that your whole makeup and personality characteristics must be recognized and accepted." This quote reminds us that a spiritual path is meant to support inclusiveness of all our traits and experiences.

One form of spiritual materialism is having the belief that possessions can relieve your suffering. For example, one might believe that when he makes enough money, he will be free of worry and anxiety. Although possessions may bring temporary happiness, the unending supply of wants only fuels the need for the next "fix." For instance, when one million dollars is acquired, the need for two million dollars emerges, and so on.

Another form of materialism is the belief that aligning yourself with a particular philosophy or spiritual group will relieve suffering. The idea is that finding the "real" path will create real and lasting harmony in your life. People who lean toward this defense might also believe that acquiring certain spiritual accomplishments will free them from future adversity. For example, a person might believe his pain and distress will be relieved by acquiring twenty years of sobriety—or by experiencing the process of kundalini awakening, by attending a ten-day meditation retreat, by completing a spiritual detox, by taking a shamanic journey, or by repeatedly working the Steps. . . . The list goes on and on.

Lastly, pursuing a particular state of mind—such as acceptance or love—with the belief that it will become a permanent refuge from suffering is a form of spiritual materialism. Attempting to maintain feelings of bliss, or peace of mind, only serves to prolong the suffering one is attempting to avoid. You can only experience happy thoughts for so long before the complexities of reality bubble up to the surface. And the good news is that the reverse is also true—you can only experience sadness for so long before some happiness rises to the surface.

It is worth noting that, although Trungpa embodied very sophisticated spiritual teachings, he also died as a practicing alcoholic. His own understanding of psychological and spiritual integration did not protect him from his own humanity. In this way, his life path exemplified the very ideas he was expressing. No amount of spiritual experience, practice, knowledge, philosophy, community, or commodity will relieve a person from the human condition. The following section will continue our exploration of relevant themes to spiritual bypass by discussing the *pre/trans fallacy*.

Half Measures Availed Us Something

Transpersonal psychology is a branch of psychology that contains all of the traditional psychological subjects while paying equal attention to the spiritual aspects of life. In *Psychotherapy and Spirit: Theory and Practice in Transpersonal Psychotherapy* by Brant Cortright, Ken Wilber is referred to as "the preeminent theoretician in transpersonal psychology." The focal point of his theory is called the *spectrum of consciousness*, which in his view encompasses all psychotherapies and spiritual traditions under one theoretical umbrella. Certainly a thorough review of Wilber's theory is beyond the scope of this book, but his concept of the pre/trans fallacy is important to our topic. At its most basic level, the pre/trans fallacy occurs when we combine early and later stages of consciousness into one stage. Most notably, we confuse the state of not knowing with the achievement of enlightenment or we muddle the purity of infancy with the wisdom and integration of adulthood. The pre/trans fallacy condenses the complexity of spiritual and psychological development into a falsely straightforward endeavor.

As background to the pre/trans fallacy, Wilber views consciousness as evolving on a developmental continuum. He calls the first stage of evolution *prepersonal*, as this is the phase of matter and nature. In the prepersonal realm, we are conscious of our senses, our bodily sensations, and our perceptions. The second stage, *personal* consciousness, relates to our mental awareness, our ego, and self-consciousness. In the personal realm, rational thought predominates. The third stage of consciousness is *transpersonal*. Since *trans* means *beyond*, in this realm we recognize our spiritual makeup as human beings. Wilber sees development as moving from "nature to humanity to divinity, from subconscious to self-conscious to super-conscious." Using Wilber's language, our consciousness evolves from prepersonal to personal to transpersonal.

The essence of the pre/trans fallacy is equating prepersonal states of consciousness with transpersonal states. The two distinct stages relating to early and advanced consciousness have been fused into one. In his article "The Pre/Trans Fallacy," Wilber explains the reason for this phenomenon:

> Since development moves from prepersonal to personal to transpersonal, and *since* both prepersonal and transpersonal are, in their own ways nonpersonal, *then* prepersonal and transpersonal tend to appear similar, even identical, to the untutored eye.

When the fallacy occurs, we seemingly have two stages of development, rather than three. While all three stages of development are still in existence, one's worldview becomes altered to fit the misperception that there are only two. This misperception has two forms: The first form involves elevating the prepersonal to the transpersonal, when a person believes all things start with the ego and move toward transcendence (leaving only the personal and transpersonal realms). The second form involves reducing the transpersonal to the prepersonal, when a person believes all things culminate with the ego (leaving only the prepersonal and personal realms). For the purposes of this book, we will look at the first form—the tendency to elevate the prepersonal to the transpersonal, or the mundane to the Divine—because this fallacy demonstrates how an addict in Twelve Step recovery might experience spiritual bypass.

One example of this form of the pre/trans fallacy can be seen in this example: if we look at a baby as representing the prepersonal stage of development, she is happy, blissful, and relatively free of troubles. The baby is conscious of her bodily sensations, namely her hunger and digestion. As she gets older, she begins to transition to the personal stage of consciousness. The task here is for the girl to develop a sense of herself and who she is in the world, to develop her ego. Lastly, the girl grows and matures to understand herself as spiritual in nature. She begins to wonder about the mysteries of life and her connection to them. Here she is in the transpersonal stage of consciousness. When the pre/trans fallacy occurs, we confuse the state of not knowing (as a baby) with the ability to know and hold the complexities of the entire spectrum. With this misunderstanding arises the expectation that transcendence (or the transpersonal stage) means never being plagued with difficulties—that one is entitled to a strictly happy and blissful existence. When a person makes this error in the context of recovery, she might believe sobriety should equal freedom from troubles or admitting powerlessness should equal transcendence. Using Wilber's model, we will continue to explore how this occurs and why making distinctions among all three realms of consciousness could be instrumental in second-stage recovery.

When a person elevates the prepersonal realm (matter and nature) to the transpersonal realm (spirituality), the prepersonal realm appears to be lost altogether. Therefore, one sees development as solely moving from personal to transpersonal, from ego to spirituality. In the absence of prepersonal consciousness, the ego appears to be the low point of human potential, while anything non-ego is glorified as Divine. Rather than a rich picture of evolution, a black-or-white model of human development is established. We see things as right or wrong, good or bad. Wilber explains that such a binary worldview misses this fact:

> The ego . . . is merely the first structure developed enough to recognize self-consciously that the world is *already* fallen from Spirit. . . . The fact that the ego can now *choose* to act toward Spirit, or choose to deny it, merely adds to the illusion that the ego's existence alone is the instigator of all alienation in the cosmos.

In other words, the ego isn't all bad or all wrong. It is actually the very thing that enables us to choose spiritual development. The ego is an evolutionary step above matter and nature in that we are capable of conscious thought. If we relate these ideas to the alcoholic in recovery, "hitting bottom" is not truly one's lowest point, as the expression suggests. The alcoholic at this stage is finally capable of recognizing alcoholism and can choose to enter recovery, enabling greater consciousness and connection to one's Higher Power. At that point, the person is actually halfway between alienation from spirit (prepersonal) and connection with spirit (transpersonal).

In this illustration, we can see that the ego is vastly undervalued when the pre/trans fallacy is operating. This same sentiment can be seen in *Twelve Steps and Twelve Traditions* as "all of A.A.'s Twelve Steps ask us to go contrary to our natural desires . . . they all deflate our egos." I would like to suggest that the pervasive devaluation of the ego is actually a barrier to lasting recovery and emotional sobriety. Meher Baba, an Indian mystic and spiritual master, emphasizes this idea in the following quote from Wilber's 1982 writing:

> The part played by the ego in human life may be compared with the function of the ballast in a ship. The ballast keeps the ship from too much oscillation; without it, the ship is likely to be too light and unsteady and in danger of being overturned.

When there are only two choices, the ego or the Divine, the ego becomes denigrated and viewed as a dispensable part of the whole person. Wilber views such denigration as the root cause of much suffering, because most people who are in need of therapy are struggling with difficulties having to do with a lack of ego or self-esteem, which he refers to as *ego-esteem*. Those who are engaged in the pre/trans fallacy are asked to let go of the very thing they need to strengthen to overcome their troubles. In other words, when the pre/trans fallacy occurs, the value of the ego and of having a strong sense of one's self is greatly diminished. Without a strong sense of one's self, obtaining greater consciousness and freedom becomes next to impossible. It is like trying to soar without wind under your wings.

An additional comment about the transpersonal realm should be included in this discussion, as Wilber believes that accessing transpersonal consciousness (spirituality) does not mean losing aspects of prepersonal and personal consciousness. Transcendence does not destroy the physical self or the capacity of the ego. He explains the concept this way: "What is negated is the exclusivity of mind; what is preserved is the capacity of mind."

Relating this to Twelve Step programs, recovery requires a connection to one's self, to others, and to something greater. Prepersonal and personal levels of consciousness are integrated within one's development. This idea is reflected in AA meetings when a member with long-term sobriety introduces himself as "My name is David, and I'm an alcoholic." He did not transcend his alcoholism, but he incorporated it into his self-concept while cultivating more consciousness about what it means to be an alcoholic in recovery.

Wilber believes that Carl Jung falls victim to the common misunderstandings inherent in the pre/trans fallacy—in which early and later stages of consciousness are erroneously combined. Wilber comments that "For Jung, there are only two major realms: the personal and the collective. He correctly and very explicitly recognizes the transpersonal or numinous dimension, but he often fuses or confuses it with prepersonal structures." Given Jung's influence on Bill Wilson and the origins of AA (chapter 3 covers this influence in detail), it would stand to reason that AA members would additionally identify with the pre/trans fallacy. One example can be found in the AA tenet "Half measures availed us nothing." In the context of Wilber's spectrum of consciousness, where all three realms are essential building blocks, reaching the halfway point is a vital step in the process. You have to go from A to B before you can go from B to C. If the pre/trans fallacy were not operating in this quote from the Big Book, it could be rewritten as "Half measures availed us half of the progress."

In Conclusion

The term *spiritual bypass* came out of Welwood's efforts to bridge Western psychology with eastern spirituality. He witnessed westerners' frustration in meditation when it didn't relieve their struggles, and he became interested in how the defense was problematic for spiritual seekers. Although the defense mechanism was discovered in the context of Eastern spiritual practice, it is not exclusive to a specific spiritual ideology or practice. The defense mechanism is more related to being human than it is to any particular faith.

The shorthand for spiritual bypass is when a person wears a mask or presents a false spiritual self that represses aspects of that person's true self. Spiritual bypass involves bolstering our defenses rather than our humility. Bypass involves grasping rather than gratitude, arriving rather than being, avoiding rather than accepting. It serves as a protection and as a roadblock momentarily, intermittently, or pervasively. As human beings, we are stuck with our flaws and our fears, but we also come with a remarkable ability to blind ourselves to things we aren't ready to see. It makes you wonder whether this capacity is a blessing or a curse. Most likely both are true, and it is rather miraculous when you think about it—we use an unconscious defense mechanism to keep ourselves unconscious.

THREE

Bill's Story Revisited

"Take an interest in your pain and your fear. Move closer, lean in, get curious; even for a moment, experience the feelings without labels, beyond being good or bad. Welcome them. Invite them. Do anything that helps melt the resistance."

— PEMA CHÖDRÖN,
WHEN THINGS FALL APART

M OST PEOPLE IN TWELVE STEP PROGRAMS have heard of Bill Wilson's story. The Big Book chronicles the depths of the fellowship co-founder's grandiose thinking, his faltering business, his relationship to alcohol, and the formation of Alcoholics Anonymous. For many individuals, the rest of Bill's story is primarily characterized by the fellowship itself. This is to say that the Steps and the literature were primarily written by Bill, he remained sober for thirty-six years until the day he died, and these are the most salient points about his life and are the legacies that he leaves behind.

Some of the lesser-known facts about Bill's life in sobriety reveal the difficulty he had living up to the principles that he wrote about so brilliantly. Ultimately, despite creating a fellowship that changed the face of alcoholism and recovery, Bill was just a human being. It is important to recognize and understand this fact, not to diminish what he brought to the world, but to puncture the notion of him as transcended after he had his spiritual experience. Bill had a profound spiritual awakening, which led to his sobriety, but he retained the essence of who he was as a man throughout his life in recovery. Drawing attention to his humanity gives individuals in recovery permission to retain their humanity as well. With information taken from several accounts of his life, let's look at Bill's story as it relates to our topic of spiritual bypass and second-stage recovery.

Bill was a progressed alcoholic. By the time he was thirty-nine, he had been hospitalized four times for his alcoholism. Both he and his wife, Lois, were losing hope that he would ever recover. It was during his last hospital stay that Bill had the spiritual experience that led to his sobriety. In *Alcoholics Anonymous Comes of Age,* he tells us how it occurred:

> My depression deepened unbearably and finally it seemed to me as though I were at the bottom of a pit. I still gagged badly on the notion of a Power greater than myself, but finally, just for the moment, the last vestige of my proud obstinacy was crushed. All at once I found myself crying out, "If there is a God, let Him show Himself! I am ready to do anything, anything!"
>
> Suddenly the room lit up with a great white light. I was caught up into an ecstasy which there are no words to describe. It seemed to me, in the mind's eye, that I was on a mountain and that a wind not of air but of spirit was blowing. And then it burst upon me that I was a free man. Slowly the ecstasy subsided. I lay on the bed, but now for a time I was in another world, a new world of consciousness. All about me and through me there was a wonderful feeling of Presence, and I thought to myself, "So this is the God of the preachers!" A great peace stole over me and I thought, "No matter how wrong things seem to be, they are all right. Things are all right with God and His World."

Bill wondered for a time whether he was experiencing some sort of brain damage, but his physician, Dr. William Duncan Silkworth, assured him that his experience was not a delirium. Silkworth believed that it was a conversion experience, a spiritual awakening. Bill was later given a copy of William

James's book *The Varieties of Religious Experience*. It helped him to understand and legitimize what had happened to him. Bill read the book cover to cover and was able to see three commonalities in the experiences written about by James: first a calamity and desperation, then an experience of true defeat, and finally an appeal to a Higher Power. Again, Bill describes it in *Alcoholics Anonymous Comes of Age*:

> Spiritual experiences, James thought, could have objective reality; almost like gifts from the blue, they could transform people. Some were sudden brilliant illuminations; others came on very gradually. Some flowed out of religious channels; others did not. But nearly all had the great common denominators of pain, suffering, calamity. Complete hopelessness and deflation at depth were almost always required to make the recipient ready. The significance of all this burst upon me. *Deflation at depth*—yes, that was *it*. Exactly that had happened to me.

Bill Wilson now had the central ingredients of the first Twelve Step program. His friend Ebby Thacher had shared his personal experience, strength, and hope—allowing Bill to gain some acceptance of his own drinking problem. Dr. Silkworth introduced Bill to the idea that alcoholism was an allergy, and now he had his personal white light experience. Alcoholics Anonymous was essentially born on this foundation: alcoholism is a disease that can be arrested one day at a time through one alcoholic talking to another about a spiritual solution to their malady.

Deepening the spiritual foundation of the burgeoning program, Wilson initiated a correspondence with the prominent Swiss psychiatrist Carl Jung. Jung referred to an alcoholic patient in one of his letters: "His craving for alcohol was the equivalent, on a low level, of the spiritual thirst of our being for wholeness, expressed in medieval language: the union with God." Jung went on to say, "Alcohol in Latin is *spiritus* and you use the same word for the highest religious experience as well as for the most depraving poison." In "A Psychological Approach to the Trinity," Jung wrote about conversion experiences such as Wilson's:

> It is clear that these changes are not everyday occurrences, but are very fateful transformations indeed. Usually they have a numinous character. . . . Modern man has such hopelessly muddled ideas about anything "mystical," or else a rationalistic fear of it, that, if ever a mystical experience should befall him, he is sure to misunderstand its true character and will deny or repress its numinousity. . . . The numinous character of these experiences is proved by the fact that they are *overwhelming*, an admission that goes not only against our pride, but against our deep-rooted fear that consciousness may perhaps lose its ascendancy.

This passage by Jung speaks to the power of spiritual transformation and to why a recovering alcoholic might fearfully avoid such an experience. Humans don't easily give up the feeling of control. For all the ways we fall short and live in an illusion of our own making, our way of being in the world is the only thing we know. Bill wanted to change this for alcoholics. He was striving to be more inclusive of all of life's offerings and to seek the next wave of brilliance and understanding. He knew that he didn't have it all figured out and he suggested we look to religious people for the ways in which they were "right." The Big Book's original version was edited to remove many of the "musts," ensuring an open and accepting feeling for alcoholics—whatever their background. Bill's spiritual experience had changed his life, and he wanted to keep his newfound sobriety by giving it to others.

As a smart businessperson, Bill knew that he was the face of Alcoholics Anonymous and that he had to play the part of a model AA member for the fellowship to thrive. If he had been publicly open about the depth of his continual suffering and the ways in which his character defects continued to drive him in sobriety, AA might not have become the movement that it is today. Bill's primary aim was to help others avoid the despair that he suffered while drinking. Without a doubt, his active alcoholism had remained far worse than any of the frailties he experienced in sobriety. But in his attempt to bring the life-saving program to other alcoholics by playing the part of a fully recovered citizen, he had been placed on a pedestal, as someone to look up to as a model of what Twelve Step programs can provide. Consequently, millions of recovering individuals have been compelled to live up to a legend that is only partially true.

While Bill's efforts to carry the message were embedded in his desire to stay sober and to help another alcoholic, he was also power driven and liked the attention he was receiving in the process. Bill wrote so eloquently about the ego because his opinion of himself was quite high. He was known for his magical thinking in the early days of AA, believing that if he took the time to share his story with a fellow drunk, the man was sure to get sober. He was so involved in the process of spreading the message that Lois was left to do the bulk of the work. In the Wilson's home, alcoholics came and went, often staying with the couple for periods of time. After a long day of earning their only steady income, Lois would do all the cooking and cleaning for Bill and their guests. She often felt left out and disregarded. One of the biggest slights she felt was when Bill wrote the chapter "To Wives" in *Alcoholics Anonymous*, the Big Book. Lois thought that she should have been given the opportunity to write about her experience as the wife of an alcoholic rather than Bill speaking on her behalf. These are just a few examples of Bill's personality remaining intact after his spiritual experience.

One of the most devastating aspects of Bill's recovery was his eleven-year battle with depression. Although he had experienced depression as an adolescent and throughout his drinking, he was five years sober before a crippling attack occurred in sobriety. The first two years of his depression were persistently bleak; Bill was often bedridden and was said to be suicidal.

In an attempt to find some relief, Bill sought the help of a psychoanalyst. For the man who created a program that promised a new freedom and a new happiness, it was an act of both desperation and courage to seek help outside of the fellowship.

For that matter, Bill sought every remedy imaginable, including multiple physical exams, osteopathic treatments, hormone replacement, thyroid remedies, B-12 vitamins, and a regimen of daily walking and breathing exercises. Many of these methods brought some relief, but none worked entirely.

Bill received criticism from other AA members and judged himself for not working a better program. He felt guilty for not living up to higher standards, which ultimately led to his desire to have a separate identity from AA. He knew it was not possible to live up to the principles that the program embodied, and yet the group needed to uphold these ideals. The group conscience in AA comes out of this knowledge, as does the guideline of "Progress, not perfection" for its members.

By going through such a debilitating depression in sobriety, Bill realized AA would not be a panacea for all that ails the alcoholic. He also discovered that alcoholism often masks underlying psychological issues. Out of this awareness, he stayed committed to continually searching for greater enlightenment above and beyond the Twelve Steps. He wanted to again experience the "fourth dimension" about which he wrote in early sobriety. He also wanted to help fellow alcoholics for whom sobriety alone was not yielding such an experience.

Along his way to greater evolution, Bill was constantly reminded that the human condition includes the necessary experience of pain. In a letter to a fellow sufferer of depression, Bill wrote, "In the long run, everything evolves for the better, not because of pleasure, but because of pain." A Jesuit priest, Father Edward Dowling, who provided spiritual counsel for Bill for more than twenty years, confirmed this idea for him. On the night they met, Bill shared about his frustrations and was curious whether there would ever be true relief. Father Dowling replied, "Never. Never any." He told Bill that "divine dissatisfaction" would be the only thing that propelled him forward and that, as he continued to aim for unrealized goals, he would discover what God actually had in store for him. Father Dowling referred to this perpetual striving as a divine thirst.

It is interesting to note that Bill wrote *Twelve Steps and Twelve Traditions* while he was in the grips of depression. His idea was to expand on the original Steps while reflecting that sobriety was an ongoing process, not an instant cure for the various disturbances that remain once an alcoholic stops drinking. Embracing his own ongoing discovery in sobriety, Bill became fascinated with the paranormal. He believed that he had psychic ability and dedicated a room in his home as a "spook room," where he conducted sessions on the ouija board, communing with the dead. Bill would act as a scribe for messages he received from the other side. He was forever invested in finding direct routes to conscious contact, including participating in experiments on precognition.

Another foray into expanding consciousness happened in 1954, when Bill was introduced to two scientists who were working on a biochemical solution to alcoholism and schizophrenia. The doctors believed they could lower the alcoholic's resistance by administering lysergic acid diethylamide (LSD). The psychedelic drug was new and unregulated, but the idea was that LSD would cause symptoms similar to delirium tremens (DTs). Since the doctors believed that DTs were an inherent part of an alcoholic's early recovery process, they wanted to induce DTs to bring about sobriety. Bill eventually became curious about these experiments and in '*Pass It On*' he wrote,

> It is a generally acknowledged fact in spiritual development that ego reduction makes the influx of God's grace possible. If, therefore, under LSD we can have a temporary reduction, so that we can better see what we are and where we are going—well, that might be of some help. The goal might become clearer. So I consider LSD to be of some value to some people, and practically no damage to anyone. It will never take the place of any of the existing means by which we can reduce the ego, and keep it reduced.

Bill began to experiment with LSD under the guidance of psychiatrists at the Los Angeles Veterans Administration Hospital. He had a spiritual experience much like his original "white light" event and he invited others to join in the experiment. Father Dowling reportedly had a positive spiritual experience with LSD, and even Lois was said to have tried a partial dose. Most AA members were opposed to experimenting with mind-altering substances, though, and there was much backlash in the AA community about the LSD trials.

Bill eventually withdrew from the experiments despite wanting to pursue them further. As co-founder of the program, he felt tethered to AA in a way that didn't allow him to have his own life and path. He was fascinated with psychic phenomena, his own experiences with the afterlife, and countless stories he had heard from other AA members. He wanted to help the pioneers of parapsychology prove that these things existed.

Although he didn't take any more LSD, he did stay in contact with the doctors performing the experiments and, under their direction, he became an advocate of taking niacin (vitamin B-3) for the emotional difficulties related to alcoholism. In this effort, Bill was seen to be breaking the Sixth Tradition of the program, as he was endorsing an outside enterprise.

Regardless of how you feel about Bill's outside interests, it is clear that the AA co-founder's own spiritual journey was somewhat limited by the spiritual program that he founded. He was striving for progress in his life, but he was continually held to specific standards of behavior by AA members and the program's critics. The irony of this begs these questions: How might current members of AA be stifled in their own unique paths? Is recovery in today's AA supportive of cultivating a personal and authentic identity or in some way limiting these? Is a person's recovery allowing the full breadth of human experience or is a bypass occurring that precludes some of the earthier nuances that might play a key role in someone's life? If pain is the touchstone to spiritual growth, are we tolerant of the sort of painful conditions that might foster such development?

When you read about Bill, there is no doubt that he was a real person, with all the shortcomings and difficulties that any of us have, before and after he got sober. The one true change for Bill was that he stayed sober. The truth is that if Bill had kept drinking, he surely would have been permanently jailed or hospitalized, or died an early death. This is where that saying comes from in AA, that alcoholics are bound for "jails, institutions, or death." Prior to recovery, Bill had truly reached the end of the line. Sobriety alone was the gift.

When you read about the advanced levels of alcoholism that the early members of AA were experiencing, it is clear that they were all at a very low bottom. They could not stop drinking and had lost everything. Perhaps the expectation that recovery should equal a "perfect health" can be linked with the arrival of "higher-bottom" alcoholics becoming sober. In other words, alcoholics with a high bottom expected a shift of equal magnitude in their own lives to what they witnessed for "low-bottom" alcoholics. The early AA stories were miraculous. Bill was putting the mattress on the bottom floor of his home so that he wouldn't jump out the window at night. For him to become sober after all he had been through was truly astounding. Who doesn't want to experience such extraordinary transformation? Perhaps sobriety alone doesn't allow such dramatic shifts.

Another reason some might believe that sobriety equals transcendence is simply wishful thinking. Just as some of the early AA members shamed Bill for his depression and for not diligently working the Steps (presumably in the hope that they would be immune to such misery as long as they were doing the "work"), this same phenomenon occurs in Twelve Step programs today. People display shadow aspects that repel us, so we tell ourselves that could never happen to us. We create rules to live by that keep us "right," follow them to the letter of the law, and cast out anyone who believes or does it differently. It is a sad truth that many of us lack compassion for others who don't see it the same as we do or who have a different experience. It is terrifying to think that we, too, could suffer a debilitating depression, that we could lose our house, or that a spouse could cheat. So we imagine our way of navigating the world will keep us safe from such things. AA members' individual makeup, coupled with a predilection for good stories with happy endings, can lead to a preference for principles that support what one wants to know. This has colored the way in which some people see their fellow AA members, even the co-founder of the program.

Bill's upswing in sobriety was clearly remarkable in that it led to Alcoholics Anonymous. However, he never quit smoking cigarettes, even after developing emphysema. In some circles, he was considered a womanizer who was unfaithful to his wife. He had an insatiable need for approval, and people who knew him well did not associate him with the word *serenity*. He struggled with insecurity and self-doubt throughout his sobriety. He was homeless for two years in recovery, having moved fifty-four times. Bill did not transcend the human condition, but he did stay sober.

He wanted people to know this distinction—between striving for spiritual enlightenment and achieving it. Much of AA was based on the Oxford Group, a Christian evangelical movement dedicated to absolute honesty, purity, unselfishness, and love; however, Bill wanted to retain the principles without the "absolutes." He knew that ideals were perfect and that human beings were not. He broke away from the Oxford Group for many reasons that allude to "progress, not perfection." Bill didn't want to tell people what to do or what to believe. He strove for inclusivity and never wanted to alienate a potential AA member.

While the intention of "principles before personalities" in AA is to retain the principles without diluting them and to welcome anyone into the program regardless of his or her personality, perhaps the downside to teasing out the personality from Bill's story was that it created an illusion of perfection. Hearing about the principles in a "general way" can mystify people who are only hearing about the "solution" in Twelve Step meetings. The Traditions that were designed to uphold the program can unintentionally set unattainable standards for members. Putting principles first can work, as long as people in recovery can simultaneously honor their own personal experience. This was

Bill's hope. He knew that recovery did not equal immunity—from further investigation, from the trials that life can bring, or from the underlying personality and psychological issues that were there before he got sober. Recovery allowed him to face these things consciously, courageously, and imperfectly.

FOUR

Spiritual Bypass and Twelve Step Recovery

"Alcohol in Latin is spiritus *and you use the same word for the highest religious experience as well as for the most depraving poison."*

— CARL JUNG

SINCE ALCOHOLICS ANONYMOUS WAS FOUNDED in 1935, it has become the most influential self-help organization in the world and has undoubtedly rehabilitated more alcoholics than the efforts of psychiatry and psychology combined. In 2007, Alcoholics Anonymous World Services Inc. reported more than two million members worldwide, which does not include membership in the many other thriving Twelve Step programs sprung from AA philosophy. Based on the US National Alcohol Survey in 1990 (as cited in an *Addiction* journal article by Room and Greenfield), it was estimated that more than 13 percent of the adult population of the United States had attended at least one Twelve Step meeting in their lifetime. Addiction specialists have written that the pioneers of AA should feel tremendously proud that the guiding principles and philosophy of their recovery movement have become so widely accepted by the medical profession and society at large. However, the high rates of relapse remain troubling, to say the least.

The foreword to the second edition of *Alcoholics Anonymous* was written in 1955 and it claimed that 75 percent of members achieved sobriety. Many decades later, the topic of relapse in AA is heavily debated. Author Toni Carter cites the rate of recovery for alcoholics in AA as 34 percent, but others say it is closer to 5 percent. The large decline in the rate of recovery over time points to the crucial issue of relapse in Twelve Step programs.

Why alcoholics in recovery return to active addiction is quite a compelling question. Although many theories address relapse prevention, the emphasis on AA's spiritual foundation points to the significance of finding a strong spiritual path to achieve sustainable recovery. As evidenced in a Tav Sparks's article referring to Bill Wilson's personal story, "the key to recovery and its absolute prerequisite is a spiritual or transpersonal awakening." Using the language of AA, a "psychic change" must occur for alcoholics to remain sober. From this perspective, anything that stands in the way of a psychic change might negatively affect one's recovery. One possible culprit in this dilemma is spiritual bypass.

How and why does a recovering person experience spiritual bypass to the extent that it precludes his recovery? The addict's personality, interpretations of AA literature, and the role of sponsorship can all contribute to one's experience of spiritual bypass.

You've Got Personality

Much research suggests that alcoholics meet the criteria for narcissism far and above the general population. The Big Book is filled with examples of narcissistic personality traits: "Selfishness—self-centeredness! That, we think, is the root of our troubles. . . . The alcoholic is an extreme example of self-will run riot, though he usually doesn't think so." Although many people think of narcissism as depicted in Greek mythology's Narcissus who could not stop staring at his own reflection, narcissism is more complex than one's love for himself. Narcissism is a personality type that ranges from mild features to a severe personality disorder. Many of these features can make one vulnerable to spiritual bypass.

Unlike Narcissus, who was content to gaze at himself in the pond, narcissists have a deep need to be validated by others and often crave the center of attention. In the extreme form, narcissism comes with an overbearing sense of entitlement and an inability to tolerate the least bit of criticism. All these traits make it tremendously difficult for someone with narcissistic personality disorder to be vulnerable enough to receive the love and acceptance he longs for. The narcissist's bravado gives him a much-needed sense of safety, but it also separates him from others. A paradox contained in narcissism is that one tends to have a high regard for himself while being defensive and desperately needy. People in AA often refer to this contradiction by sharing, "I'm an egomaniac with low self-esteem, because I can't stop thinking about myself, and I only think negative thoughts."

The defensive nature of narcissism might lead AA members to use the program as a spiritual bypass against their feelings. The need to defend one's self at all costs often occurs because a *narcissistic wound* was sustained in childhood. Basically speaking, this can occur when a child's needs are not met or are only met when the child performs in a certain way (in this case, meeting caregivers' needs rather than the child's). This wounding can lead to a pattern of trying to relate through performing or showing greatness rather than through vulnerability. The person with narcissism finds himself in a terrible bind, because he is desperate to connect but can only conceive of connection by domination or by trying to prove himself. Because vulnerability invites too much shame and humiliation, he is more likely to use spiritual tools and ideas to defend his true self than to show it to others. He might be able to articulate the spiritual aspects of the program without having an ability to personally apply them, or he might work the Steps in a way that supports a desire for invincibility rather than open-mindedness and honesty. The narcissist's attempts to protect himself can make it impossible to truly surrender, because doing so would present a terrifying opportunity to be hurt again.

To expand on the idea that narcissism allows a greater tendency for spiritual bypass, let's look at an additional aspect of narcissism: grandiosity. As characterized in *Twelve Steps and*

Twelve Traditions, "our natural disposition is inclined to self-righteousness or grandiosity." Grandiosity includes the notion that one is both unique and superior. Dr. Harry Tiebout, who was Bill Wilson's psychiatrist, has written that "grandiosity characteristically fills a person with feelings of omnipotence, demands for direct gratification of wishes, and a proneness to interpret frustration as evidence of rejection and lack of love." Just as active alcoholics sought instant gratification through their drinking, sober alcoholics can unrealistically strive to alter how they are feeling in sobriety.

Examples of people in recovery who desire instant gratification can often be found in AA. Tools such as sharing in a meeting, writing, calling a fellow program member, working a particular Step, or finding a prayer to recite are all helpful resources for people in recovery. However, when a tool is being used to maintain a self-centered stance, it is not being used in an act of surrender, but in an act of grandiose thinking. An example of using the tools narcissistically is when someone shares in a meeting by telling others what to do, rather than by coping with her own concerns. This might be due to her intolerance of personal frustration (for the fear that it solidifies her feelings of unworthiness) and so she must defend against her own struggle and speak about what *you* should do when you are uncomfortable. This allows her an opportunity to be seen and heard, but rather than soothing underlying hurt, it amplifies her feeling of superiority.

The same personality traits that aided someone in justifying her drinking or using can be barriers to seeing herself clearly when she is sober. One's personality is like a lens through which she perceives the world, and the inherent blind spots are inroads to defenses, such as spiritual bypass. It is a painful reality that recovering alcoholics often have to face deep personal traumas when they get sober. In addition, they have to uncover the various ways that they remain committed to concealing their wounding throughout recovery. The hope that spiritual practice might allow a person to avoid facing such pain might sustain sobriety for a time, but it is just another bandage and may lead to relapse rather than recovery.

Reading between the Lines

When Bill Wilson and the original members of AA came together to discuss the Twelve Steps and the principles they wanted to incorporate into the program, their aim was to focus on a pathway toward an authentic spiritual awakening. Reflections of this intention can be found in *Alcoholics Anonymous*:

> We have come to believe He would like us to keep our heads in the clouds with Him, but that our feet ought to be firmly planted on earth. That is where our fellow travelers are, and that is where our work must be done.

Another example is "We claim spiritual progress rather than spiritual perfection." Both passages are indicative of striving for spiritual principles while acknowledging one's fallibility as a human being. However, several passages in AA literature might be used to support spiritual bypass. For example, the following quote might lead someone to think that he should not be responsible for his thoughts and actions:

> When we saw others solve their problems by a simple reliance upon the Spirit of the Universe, we had to stop doubting the power of God. Our ideas did not work. But the God idea did.

Another reference, "spiritual principles would solve all my problems," could be read as endorsing spiritual bypass by claiming that all difficulties can be solved through spirituality. In both cases, spiritual bypass is seemingly condoned if one does not read the passages in context and in conjunction with the rest of the outlined program. This is one critical juncture at which encouraging an alcoholic to "take what you like and leave the rest," as is often suggested, might lead to spiritual bypass.

Addicts tend to have an expectation that they should feel good all of the time. When someone with this belief reads

The Promises (found in *Alcoholics Anonymous*, pages 83–84), they are offered assurance that feeling good all the time is achievable. This, of course, is not the case—which could prove confusing at best when it comes to interpreting The Promises:

> If we are painstaking about this phase of our development, we will be amazed before we are halfway through. We are going to know a new freedom and a new happiness. We will not regret the past nor wish to shut the door on it. We will comprehend the word *serenity* and we will know peace. No matter how far down the scale we have gone, we will see how our experience can benefit others. That feeling of uselessness and self-pity will disappear. We will lose interest in selfish things and gain interest in our fellows. Self-seeking will slip away. Our whole attitude and outlook upon life will change. Fear of people and of economic insecurity will leave us. We will intuitively know how to handle situations which used to baffle us. We will suddenly realize that God is doing for us what we could not do for ourselves.
>
> Are these extravagant promises? We think not. They are being fulfilled among us—sometimes quickly, sometimes slowly. They will always materialize if we work for them.

The Promises paint a solely positive picture of recovery, even going so far as to say they will "always materialize" if one works for them. This can lead a person in recovery to feel as though he is doing something wrong if he is not experiencing every promise. In other words, if someone is feeling sad or angry, he might believe that he is not working a successful program. He could mistake the absence of "happy, joyous, and free" feelings as evidence that he is missing something vital in his recovery. If someone is afraid, he might think he isn't "turning it over" enough. The truth is that we are meant to know and experience the full range of human emotions. Sadness and fear are healthy expressions and essential guideposts for what we are going through. Experiencing these feelings is just as much a "gift" of the program as "happy, joyous, and free"—because sobriety gives people the opportunity to experience all of their feelings and to make choices about how they wish to navigate life with an abundant consciousness. Most recovering alcoholics drank with an underlying desire to mask their feelings, so the opportunity to experience the broad spectrum of human emotions can be perceived as one of the most valuable aspects of sobriety.

In addition to the Big Book passages that can be read as endorsing spiritual bypass, some sections in *Twelve Steps and Twelve Traditions* can be misconstrued. In particular, Step Ten—"Continued to take personal inventory and when we were wrong promptly admitted it"—contains language that might support one's rejection of his emotions. In an effort to encourage people in recovery to take regular inventory, and to highlight what can happen when one is unaware of what he is feeling and how it is operating, Step Ten comes across as rather rigid about what are acceptable and unacceptable emotions. Anger is discussed as a "luxury of more balanced people" that will certainly lead to a bender for the alcoholic. Jealousy, envy, and pride are considered "disturbances" rather than feelings and are considered equal predictors of relapse.

Of course, the idea embedded in Step Ten is that resentments can—and do—lead to relapse. What the reading does not address is that people will never be free of their feelings. Inventory can reveal what a person feels, as well as his "part" in the matter. Occasionally, such understanding will eliminate the fear or anger altogether. Other times, inventory will reveal both a person's feelings and her part, and it does not diminish the situation or the feelings that coincide as much as one hopes or believes that it will. In this case, the recovering person need not beat up himself for having a human experience. He can learn to tolerate his feelings, make sane and healthy choices about how to navigate them, and find ways to not drink or use *no matter what*.

The idea of long-term sobriety is to wear life like a loose-fitting garment, not to strip away the garment or to wear it like a straitjacket! In this we can be comforted by the program's tenet of "Progress, not perfection." One of the advantages of long-term sobriety is the experience of having moved through a host of thoughts and feelings that eventually came to pass. Although the program occurs "one day at a time," it is the culmination of time that enables a person to withstand and accept sadness, anger, fear, humiliation, and other difficult emotions as transient, temporary, and human. The adage "This too shall pass" is just as appropriate for experiencing The Promises as it is for experiencing their absence.

An additional observation on anger is that the Big Book was written primarily by men. Bill Wilson was the principal author, but he had much help from the other early members of the program. It is important to keep this in mind, because gender roles are deeply embedded in AA literature. Although it certainly doesn't apply to all women, the truth is that many women have been acculturated to reject their anger. For these women, getting in touch with anger can be a very healthy step in sobriety, because unexpressed anger can be turned inward as depression or self-hatred, which can lead to relapse just as much as acting out in anger can. Of course, the same could be said for men who were given a similar upbringing or outlook. John Welwood acknowledges that although compassion is a higher spiritual ideal, if it is based on rejection of one's anger, it is not genuine compassion. Genuine compassion comes when anger has been acknowledged and processed.

We cannot decide to keep a lid on certain emotions while we freely feel and express others. We are not capable of that sort of precision. To have access to all of our feelings, we need to give all of them the attention they deserve. Recovery does not afford alcoholics the ability to disassociate from their feelings but rather the ability to feel and express feelings appropriately and compassionately. If recovery is built on a person's attempt to separate himself from pain, using the literature to support this vision, relapse might very well be a necessary inoculation once again.

Carrying the Message

A sponsor can provide a personal, modern translation of the program to the newcomer who has difficulty deciphering some of the literal interpretations of AA literature. As cited in Daniel Csanyi's article on religious development, Methodist minister and professor James Fowler used the term *sponsor* in his writings on faith:

> A sponsor is one who stands beside, or walks with, us in development. The sponsor confirms our worth and expresses confidence in our potential. A sponsor will also confront and challenge us as well as propose (or exemplify) models by which we can develop.

This definition contains the spirit in which sponsorship in AA was founded. A pamphlet titled *Questions & Answers on Sponsorship*, distributed by Alcoholics Anonymous World Services Inc., states that sponsorship is when "an alcoholic who has made some progress in the recovery program shares that experience on a continuous, individual basis with another alcoholic who is attempting to attain or maintain sobriety."

Sponsorship has proven a valuable tool in AA, but it carries intrinsic complexities. As the adage indicates, "The student can only go so far as the teacher." A sponsee is at the mercy of his sponsor's interpretation of AA's Twelve Steps. In this regard, if a sponsor uses spiritual tools and ideas to bypass her wounding, she is likely to pass this tactic on through sponsorship. Thomas Merton, one of the most influential Catholic authors of the twentieth century, wrote of such a risk in *New Seeds of Contemplation*:

> He who attempts to act and do things for others and for the world without deepening his own self-understanding, freedom, integrity, and capacity to love, will not have anything to give others. He will communicate to them only the contagion of his own obsessions, his aggressiveness, his ego-centered ambitions, his delusions about ends and means, and his doctrinaire prejudices and ideas.

The insidious nature of spiritual bypass can corrupt even the basic foundation on which AA was built: one alcoholic talking to another.

One example of this phenomenon occurs when a sponsee is experiencing difficult feelings and the response from her sponsor is a blanket solution often offered in AA. For example, a sponsee might be feeling alienated in a meeting and doesn't want to continue attending what was once her home group. She brings this concern to her sponsor, who simply responds for her to "Pray about it." Certainly, prayer might bring some relief and guidance, but such a suggestion could be interpreted as avoidance. The sponsor was not interested in being present to the turmoil her sponsee was experiencing, and she therefore asked her sponsee to potentially avoid it, too, by praying for the difficulty to go away. Such suggestions might foster the experience of spiritual bypass rather than acceptance of the issues that a person is bound to face in recovery. Other blanket responses in the program include "What Step are you working on?" or "Go call three other recovering alcoholics and ask them how they are doing."

These are not inherently poor suggestions. The point is that if they are given or received with a spirit of avoidance, they are more likely in the service of spiritual bypass than in the service of a spiritual solution.

In Conclusion

The Twelve Steps were designed to help alcoholics experience the psychic change that Bill Wilson had during his hospitalization. As stated in *Twelve Steps and Twelve Traditions*, "AA's Twelve Steps are a group of principles, spiritual in their nature, which, if practiced as a way of life, can expel the obsession to drink and enable the sufferer to become happily and usefully whole." Although working the Steps *can* bring about a psychic change, it is not a guarantee. Tav Sparks, an addiction therapist, wrote about the difference between working a program that brings about a psychic change and working a program that might not:

> Exoterically, AA [ensures] physical abstinence, certain levels of surrender to the condition of alcoholism, and the need for help and group participation. It also stresses the necessity for moral, behavioral, and attitudinal adjustments through aid of a Higher Power.
>
> However, at some point . . . the seeker reaches a threshold, a dimension doorway into an ever deeper hall of humanness. He may pass through it, providing he is willing to undergo the profound death such a crossing entails and wants more than anything to answer the call toward wholeness. This is esoteric AA, the "fourth dimension" of which Bill W. wrote and the real journey toward full restoration of humanity.

The difference between exoteric and esoteric AA participation might be likened to the difference between initial sobriety and a full recovery for the alcoholic. Certainly, sobriety includes abstinence from alcohol, but recovery from the disease must also include spiritual and psychological fitness: trust, belief, and an experience of connection, coupled with the ability to acknowledge and feel all of one's feelings. This distinction must be considered when looking at the problem of relapse, particularly because it presents an entryway into the investigation of how spiritual bypass could be getting in the way of one's ongoing, or second-stage, recovery.

FIVE

Bradford

"Maybe I can postpone dealing with some of my problems indefinitely. Of course, this won't do. Such a bluffing of oneself will have to go the way of many another pleasant rationalization."

— TWELVE STEPS AND TWELVE TRADITIONS

WHAT FOLLOWS ARE THE HIGHLIGHTS from an interview I conducted with Bradford in which we aimed to capture his personal experience of spiritual bypass in recovery. At the time of our discussion, he was thirty-five years old, was married with children, and had been sober for thirteen years.

I GREW UP IN A DEVOUTLY CATHOLIC FAMILY, very traditional, but also very mystical. Mom, being from Eastern Europe, was Orthodox Catholic, but very much about the saints, Mary, intercessions, and the family history I was raised with about the miracles of the escape of, you know, somehow getting to this country with the Virgin Mary's help. So that idea of miracles, that anything is possible with God, was very much a part of it. I would say that in my upbringing with struggling with drinking, not realizing it was alcoholism, and wondering why things happen, I saw coming to AA as sort of a fruition of past prayers. I felt like I had that idea of a rebirth. But it almost immediately was different in the sense that I was very much over any idea that there was one single way, you know? I was fine going to

Catholic church with my family, I was fine calling myself a Catholic, but I saw myself transcending beyond that. It was a cultural identity more than a religious prescription.

I always felt like a black sheep growing up, as kind of the problem child, you know. My brother was straight A's, Dartmouth, Phi Beta Kappa, Notre Dame Law School, a high-powered lawyer. My sister was Vassar, law school, doctor. And then there was me—drunk, got sober in college, and then seemed to be successful. But they all followed the ultra-Catholic "live and die by the Pope" stuff. So I think I have felt, especially from my mom, like I had betrayed her . . . not betrayed her, but she expressed her disappointment that I wasn't practicing Catholicism.

When Bradford became sober in college, he watched his life "go from fucked up to really starting to look good. I was gaining a comfort level within myself and the ability to be successful, to attend classes." In his early sobriety, he "was really hungry to be normal, to be a good kid, to say I was going to do something and do it." He believed that, if he worked a good program, he would be afforded that experience. He sought to be a perfect AA member by aligning with "the Big Book fundamentalists" who read the book word for word, placing emphasis on every "must" in the text. This early introduction to AA gave Bradford a great understanding and appreciation for the literature and, additionally, filled him with hope. However, he now recognizes that *Alcoholics Anonymous,* the Big Book, is fallible and "not a bible speaking *the* truth." Additionally, he realizes that reading the book as specific, literal directions allowed him to beat himself up and point the finger at others for "not doing it right." This latter experience is one example of spiritual materialism— believing that aligning himself with a particular philosophy, point of view, or spiritual group would relieve his suffering and that acquiring certain spiritual accomplishments or possessions would free him from any pain or distress. As you will see, spiritual materialism is evidenced throughout Bradford's recovery.

At five years in the program, Bradford wanted more than sobriety and primarily focused on material success. He vigorously applied the principle of taking contrary action, which initially provided him with the results he was seeking. He judged other AA members for solely obtaining sobriety, and he was personally afraid of not living up to the high standards of wealth and achievement set by his family. At this stage of Bradford's recovery, he viewed physical, emotional, and spiritual sobriety as merely the minimum requirements of working a solid program.

Bradford wanted an accessible, straightforward path to spirituality that was consistent with his desire to manifest success and wealth. He ultimately found a religion that fit with this goal. It was at this point in his recovery that Bradford conflated spirituality with material success, which perpetuated his spiritual materialism:

> I STARTED GETTING INTO WHAT I WOULD CALL holistic religions right around five years of sobriety. I got really money-motivated, and success-oriented, and I didn't want to be the guy who just has sobriety, you know, who just goes to lots of meetings and is really active in the program but doesn't have those things. I was in grad school and even though I was a very well-paid grad student, I was tired of not having money. Through recovery I got into other self-help stuff like Tony Robbins, Napoleon Hill, anything about bettering oneself. So I guess more pop psychology, the real deep psychology stuff, and deep spiritual books really didn't interest me. So I went to a Tony Robbins seminar and I started meeting more people, and that is how I got turned onto Agape [New Thought-Ancient Wisdom Church in Los Angeles], which seemed like a perfect fit, all of a sudden making religion fit into this personal-development, kind of success-oriented model. So I did that for several years and then that really opened me up to the idea that it is all about practices.

Fusing spiritual development with financial gain has the potential to devalue the importance of a Higher Power while inflating one's sense of influence over a desired outcome. In Bradford's case, he started to view prayer as an opportunity for acquisition rather than connection. Talking to God was less about being open to direction and more about tapping into a storehouse of his wants and needs. "There is this constant frequency out there broadcasting what you need and what you want that we close ourselves off to," Bradford explained. This is an example of how he unconsciously used spiritual bypass to avoid his feelings of inadequacy and powerlessness while he started to become successful in the material world.

> I WAS ON THIS SUCCESS PATH and had started accomplishing those goals I had set when I was newly sober. All of a sudden I had what I thought was the appropriate net worth. I thought I was on a path to ultimate financial freedom, whatever that was supposed to mean. But I was also getting internally very discontent. I was wanting something more and not finding it in my corporate job. Even though I had sort of met my goals and had set new ones, there was a huge disparity now between the old goal and the new goal. Doing the things related to the old goal just wasn't interesting. So I really kind of threw myself out there and I bought a house and moved out of our condo, so that felt really good to me. And so I'm putting it together now. It is like my spirituality very much became about, like, the evidence of my spirituality was my manifestation of material things, so I had definitely conflated those.

Bradford could only see what he did *not* have and he propelled himself toward obtaining it. During this time, he used the AA adage "Act as if" as a panacea for all of the underlying emotional issues he did not want to address. A simple definition of "acting as if" is when someone acts in a way that is incongruous with how he feels, sometimes taking an action even if he does not want to. In other words, he "acts as if" the feeling and action are aligned. "Acting as if" has its place in recovery: a sober alcoholic needs to be able to function in the world such that she behaves in relationships in ways that are not damaging. An example is withholding the desire to speak inappropriately to one's boss. However, in Bradford's case, "acting as if" was an expression of spiritual bypass—avoiding his emotional pain by taking spiritual actions—and it did not give him the freedom he was seeking.

Bradford's conflation of the spiritual with the material allowed him to honor his desire for "something more," but solely through the material plane. Therefore, the only way to pursue spiritual development was to acquire more wealth. This led to detrimentally grandiose financial decisions and an inflated sense of self that had Bradford thinking he no longer needed AA.

I BECAME A CO-OWNER OF AN ART GALLERY in Beverly Hills. I ended up just being a horrible business partner. I was totally out of my head about what I could achieve. Also, I just spent a shitload of money. The experience really took my ego down, because all of a sudden I had this identity of being a gallery owner, and then not having that and not being success-ful—so kind of "Who am I?" type things.

But to put this in spiritual terms, I think what happened is that I used these spiritual things to cover up, and I have really had to confront that. I feel like a newcomer again. During this period I should say, when the twins came, I really stopped going to meetings. I wasn't active in recovery at all. And I think part of that was the ego telling me there was nothing for me to learn in AA. And the tools I was using were not AA tools, so I wasn't a good sponsor. Because what I'd want to be sponsoring people on wasn't really AA fundamentals; it was kind of like Success 101—that was what I was into. So when I looked at these people who had all this time and were like the gurus and still living in the same apartment for twenty years, I was judging them. Right, I was like, "What do you know?"

Bradford can now see that materialism is often used in the self-help arena as a seductive hook to attract people to apply spiritual principles. This was the case for him.

> WHAT I HAVE COME TO REALIZE IS THAT — this is my inter-
> pretation — the world, in order to attract us to apply
> these spiritual principles, things like *The Secret*, Tony Robbins,
> and others, uses the material, because we live in a material
> world, and that is the hook. But you end up having to do a lot
> of emotional work to attain those things. Yet, the manifestation
> of those things can happen without any spiritual growth and
> can be mistaken for spiritual growth.

Although his goal of manifesting material wealth was initially supported by emotional and spiritual growth, he eventually mistook his financial stability as evidence of stability in all areas of his life, and he abandoned his emotional and spiritual pursuits. As he describes it, he "used self-help stuff to pump myself up rather than deal with a specific emotion." This is another example of how Bradford experienced spiritual bypass.

Bradford was surprised at how "hooked" he was on material striving. He was very interested in being perceived a certain way by people in his life, and apparent wealth provided the illusion he needed to manage people's perceptions. He felt that money and success allowed him to portray perfection. This portrayal ultimately had Bradford disregarding his true feelings and his true self.

> I CAN'T SHIELD MYSELF FROM UNDERLYING FEELINGS
> because I've got money, you know? Like driving the nice
> car, and I just bought the house, and I have got my kids in
> private school, and all of that stuff that I can sort of project out

there that everything is fine. I can see how money and consumption are drugs in that way. You know, they allowed me to not have to deal with any of my own insecurities or the "Who am I?" question.

As Bradford's life continued to grow and change, he began to realize he did not have all of the tools to handle it. His "spiritual ideals" were not helping him in his daily experience. He acknowledges that it was easy for him, and he believes it is common in AA, to find something other than alcohol to compensate for underlying insecurities. In his case, striving for material success kept him stagnant in recovery. Consequently, he often felt like a fraud and was ashamed of not living up to people's expectations. It was at this point that he recognized he was using spirituality to cover up, rather than as a vehicle to continue evolving. He was seeking instant gratification, rather than acknowledging his painful feelings. If he was going to remain sober, he would eventually have to shed the defenses of spiritual bypass and spiritual materialism.

I'M REALIZING HOW MUCH ANXIETY I HAVE. I never realized how much anxiety I have . . . how much fear is really underneath a lot of what I do. I'm in constant fear of things not turning out right, or of getting caught, even when I'm not doing something wrong—but getting caught doing something that people might perceive as wrong. I'm realizing how much of a people pleaser I am. These are things I never wanted to acknowledge. Like when I got sober, I just wanted to act my way out of them just by being the strong person, just being the charming, good-looking guy. I really went from being outsider drunk to learning how to act as if, and getting really good at that. But that doesn't address the underlying . . . there was something there from being a kid where I didn't feel like I belonged. I felt fearful of what I did and as though if you knew something about me, it would be used against me.

For a period of a couple years, Bradford stopped going to meetings. He also stopped his spiritual practice, stopped working out and eating healthfully, and started to smoke cigarettes again. He understands how other people in recovery can relapse by seeing how quickly he slid back into his smoking habit. Although he did not consciously start smoking or eating to relieve his suffering, Bradford was not doing the practices that had previously helped him to stay in touch with his personal truth. When Bradford does the spiritual and emotional work that recovery asks of him (particularly being honest and open with himself and others about how he is feeling), he is not willing to pick up a cigarette.

After years of finding his sense of self and identity through his title and net worth, Bradford experienced a "gift of desperation" (G.O.D.). He was in great financial difficulty and could not handle it on his own. He felt defeated and questioned who he really was. This financial "bottom" in sobriety ultimately led to a new surrender in the program, during which Bradford became vulnerable and open to new direction.

After hitting this new bottom in recovery, Bradford remembered that abstaining from drinking or using drugs one day at a time is what makes him a success. He was reminded about the insidiousness and insanity of his addiction. Despite the fact that he was feeling good, he had lost touch with his authentic self, which includes his tendency toward addiction. This had made him feel that he could smoke a cigar without penalty, but the reality was that he eventually progressed to smoking a pack of cigarettes a day.

Coming out of this "wreckage" had Bradford feeling as if he were a newcomer again. In this sense, his bypass served as a stage of spiritual development that led to a deeper surrender and a new beginning. Bradford uses AA verbiage regarding the "road narrowing" to describe how he felt called into action to stay sober and to evolve spiritually and emotionally. He sees how avoiding the call to continue humbly working his program—showing up exactly as he was—could have eventually led to relapse with alcohol.

Just before his thirteenth AA anniversary, Bradford went back to meetings where he heard other people with long-term sobriety talking about their difficulties.

> I STARTED REALLY GETTING INVOLVED AND FINDING, you know, it is okay for me to say how fucked up I feel and how fucked up my life is—to be able to say that at twelve, thirteen years sober, and be okay with it, because I'm still sober. I don't have a desire to drink and I don't want to get high. Reminding myself that no matter what else happens, this makes me successful, right? That I'm not drinking and using. And I think there is a wonderful aspect of AA that really is about nothing else matters.

Bradford distinguishes between AA meetings at which people with long-term sobriety are sharing their truth as it is happening and the AA meetings with speakers who "pitch" their story, predominantly highlighting the positive aspects of their experience. "When you go to big speaker meetings with people with twenty, thirty years, they will tell you the ups and downs, but it is always like an overall high," he explains. "You don't ever get to see them experience the real dark moments." As part of his re-entry into AA, he had to get honest. He knew that he had to share exactly what he did not want people to know about him. By doing this, he reconnected with his vulnerability and fallibility as a recovering alcoholic. It was through sharing his truth that he found some relief and freedom. By being honest about his situation, he was able to answer the "Who am I?" question by knowing that he is *not* his career or his monetary wealth. This exercise of speaking honestly at meetings was a healthy application of taking contrary action in recovery.

> I THINK THAT IS THE GREATEST GIFT OF SOBRIETY: when things come up, I can identify them. I was in a meeting and I went like this [moved foot] and I looked at my shoes and

I got pissed. Because I had taken them to a shoe shine place and they did a great job of getting rid of the scuffs and everything, like they really used super glue or something to smooth them out because I had dinged them. But they were Prada and they had the red stripe in the back, but they fucking put black on it, you know, and you can't see the red stripe, and it's like "What good are fucking Prada loafers if everyone doesn't know you are wearing Prada loafers?" And to be able to catch myself and just laugh.

At thirteen years sober, Bradford is going back to basics. He recognizes that he has worked on these aspects of recovery in the past but that "there is a new level of work that seems to need to be done." Part of that work is to tease spiritual development and material success apart from one another. Bradford realizes that when spirituality and materialism are separated, spirituality can cease being a compensatory factor and can start to hold him in whatever circumstance he is in with the feeling that "it's all right." By separating the spiritual from the material, Bradford can make choices and recognize that they do not define him in a larger sense. He additionally finds that spirituality can be the antidote to his insecurities, as opposed to materialism, which only covers up those insecurities.

The essence of AA for Bradford is about connection to other people, to a Higher Power, and to himself. By finding nurturing connections with other people, he has been able to find connection to Spirit. While he originally sought a connection to a Higher Power through church, he ultimately found it when he accessed his own humanity. It has been through confronting his darkest truths and experiences, not overcoming them, that Bradford has been able to feel a conscious contact with God. Darkness and light have become two sides of the same coin. Bradford now accepts that the human condition includes having a dark side.

EVERYBODY HAS A DARK SIDE. Everybody has secrets. Everybody has things they do that they don't want published on the front page of the newspaper. And that isn't cynical. We are just all human.

Instead of feeling that he is doing something wrong if he isn't on top of his game, Bradford now turns to his spiritual practice for comfort. Spirituality helps him stay centered on who he truly is. Meditation serves as an opportunity to practice Step Three by turning over everything on his mind to his Higher Power. For Bradford, the ocean provides concrete evidence of something bigger into which he can release his every thought. When he is surfing, he has the ability to surrender and recognize that the tenet "To thine own self be true" has nothing to do with titles or materialism.

With regard to his emotional and psychological recovery, Bradford knew early on that addressing these facets was instrumental for his spiritual development and overall sobriety. He has returned to doing this work by being "honest, open-minded, and willing." He has acknowledged that despite a wonderful experience in recovery when he felt free of his insecurities for some time, the core feelings he experienced as a child are still within him.

THERE IS THIS LITTLE BOY who just didn't get something growing up. And not to say that people were supposed to provide it, but this is just stuff I have been avoiding. Like some of these emotions are very familiar and that is what makes them so strange . . . that I had such a long period without them, like my experience in sobriety has been so amazing that to then go back to these very core emotional feelings and, you know, self-worth and depression and things that I very distinctly remember growing up. I think they have always been there, but I overcompensated. Early in sobriety I was going to do everything perfectly. I wanted to do it right. And I think that was also just being scared.

Bradford is redefining his success from earning a certain income to being comfortable with himself at any given moment. In AA terms, he is shifting from an "outside job" to an "inside job." Emotional and psychological growth is now centered on knowing the little boy who remains inside—not to overcome him, but to acknowledge and learn how to deal with the sadness that remains. Bradford now feels that he is "enough" and believes that his overreliance on spirituality to manifest a particular income did not enable him to cope with his insecurities. He is experiencing unconditional love of self and true humility to the point that he embodies AA's idea of being "right size."

It was upon reflection during our interview that Bradford was able to recognize his spiritual bypass and spiritual materialism. He did not think he was using spiritual tools to cover up his feelings while he was doing it. Now he can see that spiritual bypass appeared to be a kinder alternative to facing his depression and feelings of worthlessness. In the end, Bradford does not see his experience with spiritual bypass as negative, particularly as it compares with using chemicals to change the way he was feeling. He sees the cyclical nature of spiritual development and is grateful that he was given the opportunity for a new surrender.

SIX

The Softer Side of Spiritual Bypass

"Spirituality involves first seeing ourselves truly, as the paradoxical and imperfect beings that we are, and then discovering that it is only within our very imperfection that we can find the peace and serenity that is available to us."

— ERNEST KURTZ AND KATHERINE KETCHAM,
THE SPIRITUALITY OF IMPERFECTION

HAVING REVIEWED DEFINITIONS for spiritual bypass and the reasons addicts in Twelve Step recovery might be prone to experiencing the defense, let's now look at spiritual bypass through the lens of developmental theory. From this perspective, spiritual bypass can be seen not just as a pitfall on one's journey, but as a natural occurrence in a person's pursuit of spiritual depth and maturity. We will begin looking at the softer side of spiritual bypass by reviewing James Fowler's and M. Scott Peck's models of spiritual development.

You Gotta Have Faith: Fowler's Six-Stage Model

As a Methodist minister and professor, James Fowler developed a six-stage model regarding the development of faith. His ideas, outlined in his book *Stages of Faith,* support the notion that spiritual bypass is a common component in healthy development. We'll consider in this section how the stages relate to spiritual bypass and Twelve Step recovery. As an introduction to his work, let's look at one way in which Fowler defines faith:

A coat against nakedness . . . faith functions so as to screen off the abyss of mystery that surrounds us. . . . Faith helps us form a dependable "life space," an ultimate environment. At a deeper level, faith undergirds us when our life space is punctured and collapses, when the felt reality of our ultimate environment proves to be less than ultimate.

This quote explains the function of faith as creating a sense of safety in an unsafe world. It is interesting to note that the description additionally resembles what one might observe when an alcoholic first lands in recovery. When someone hits bottom, his environment is punctured and collapsed. For recovery to become possible, he often relies on faith in his newfound community (G.O.D. = group of drunks) or in another personal conception of a Higher Power in which he feels supported enough to safely abandon his drug of choice.

Fowler believes that the development of faith begins when we are infants through our relationship with our caregivers. Our first conception of a Higher Power is truly the person(s) taking care of us as children. Faith, according to Fowler, "grow(s) through our experience of trust and fidelity—and of mistrust and betrayal—with those closest to us." In other words, faith is developed through the infant's ability to trust that she will be fed and held, or through the absence of such necessities. This key relationship becomes the infant's template for having faith in anything or anyone.

When this theory is applied to recovery for alcoholics, early sobriety might mirror the experience of infancy. Consider the parallel that can be made between a sober alcoholic and his Higher Power on the one hand and an infant and his caregiver on the other. People often equate recovery with a new beginning, when it becomes necessary to let go of old patterns and ideas and to allow others to love them until they are capable of loving themselves—a common adage in AA. In this sense, a newcomer is experiencing a regression in which it becomes possible to integrate new ways of relating to himself and to the world around him. The person has a second chance at developing relationships and coping mechanisms that don't require alcohol to numb the pain. He has a second chance to cultivate the type of faith that can be life-saving. This is obviously one area where the Twelve Step approach of encouraging members to cultivate a relationship with a Higher Power is a very powerful one.

Fowler's six stages of faith development allow us to see how faith might evolve over time, from an intuitive-projective stage through mythic-literal, synthetic-conventional, individuative-reflective, conjunctive faith, and universalizing stages. His model depicts faith as an ongoing process rather than something you have or you don't have. Throughout the stages, someone has many opportunities to experience spiritual bypass as an adaptive defense mechanism that can occur in a way that is supportive of an overall healthy spiritual path in recovery.

Stage 1: Intuitive-Projective

Stage 1 is called intuitive-projective. In this stage, one is very egocentric and incapable of holding multiple perspectives on an issue. When faced with having to choose a viewpoint, a person tends to perceive only the most positive aspects of a topic. Recovering people in Fowler's first stage of faith development will find it almost impossible to see that having a "life beyond their wildest dreams" lies right beside taking personal moral inventories and making amends to others for wrongs done. Spiritual bypass is likely to occur in this stage for this reason. If a person is only focused on the positive, she is automatically blind to the shadow and therefore defending against it. All work in recovery is focused on obtaining greater joy and abundance in this stage.

Another aspect of Stage 1 is the development of self-awareness and imagination. One begins to draw on personal experiences, as well as stories about religion and God, to create a comprehensive image of the world. This image shapes the way in which a person acts and responds, using newfound faith as a vehicle for initiative. Regarding spiritual bypass, an individual in Stage 1 might choose fragments from religious stories that support his belief in a Higher Power who removes all stressors from life. Seen from a developmental perspective, the belief that God is protecting a person from worry or frustration might allow sobriety to take root and for ego-strength to build. Eventually, the capacity to integrate aspects of his Higher Power emerges, allowing the individual to take appropriate responsibility for his psychological health. In the language of AA, this is where a recovery of mind, body, and spirit becomes possible.

Stage 2: Mythic-Literal

To transition to Stage 2, a person must develop the capacity to discern between "what is real and what only seems to be." Stage 2 is called mythic-literal because in this stage a person tends to have a literal take on reality. She has a tendency for black-and-white thinking, which produces "overcontrolling, stilted perfectionism or 'works righteousness.'" A recovering alcoholic in Stage 2 will tend to see herself and others as either "good" or "bad." Spiritual bypass will likely occur because she cannot tolerate personal deficiencies because she believes these will automatically negate what is worthy or right. Although such a belief might help to maintain physical sobriety for a time, Stage 2 is ultimately an impossible predicament, and sustained recovery in AA will most likely require a transition to Stage 3.

Stage 3: Synthetic-Conventional

Stage 3 is called synthetic-conventional. Members of the general population will find themselves in this category. The overarching virtue here is conformity, but a person in Stage 3 also acquires a greater capacity for critical thinking. She finds her identity by conforming to the ideal that the culture puts forth. To remain in this stage, she must remain ignorant of everything that is incongruent with the cultural norms. Fowler writes, "At Stage 3 a person has an 'ideology,' a more or less consistent clustering of values and beliefs, but he or she has not objectified it for examination and in a sense is unaware of having it." As we've discussed, if a recovering person takes on a sponsor's ideology without the ability to reflect on it, he may not be getting the complete message of the program. This is also what prompts some critics of AA to speak of the program as a "cult" because people in recovery seem to lose the ability to think for themselves. It is important to realize that conformity on a personal or collective level has a place in the development of faith and that this experience is not a stopping point. Spiritual bypass as complete compliance with a sponsor or the program may provide a person with a solid foundation on which he can build a more personal and holistic program. A transition out of Stage 3 occurs when the cognitive dissonance—the discomfort that arises when holding contradictory ideas—between conformity and critical thinking becomes too much to hold.

Stage 4: Individuative-Reflective

Stage 4 is called individuative-reflective. With this stage comes a time of deconstruction and disillusionment. An individual in Stage 4 is willing to be ejected from the Stage 3 community with its cultural norms, but the pain of such ejection can be great. For a recovering person, this stage might be an opportunity for spiritual bypass—or even for relapse, if she cannot accept the "burden of responsibility for his or her own commitments, lifestyle, beliefs, and attitudes." Spiritual bypass can occur here if she uses spirituality to deny the burden of responsibility and feelings of disillusionment. To progress through the defense, as Fowler explains, she must recognize "that life is more complex than Stage 4's logic of clear distinctions and abstract concepts can comprehend." When this occurs, the person will be propelled into Stage 5.

Stage 5: Conjunctive Faith

Conjunctive faith is Stage 5. In this remythologizing stage, a person recognizes that all Stage 3 elements are real but are metaphors for something much larger than the concretized earlier versions. In this sense, a person reappropriates values and beliefs, with room for mystery and for the unconscious. Stage 5 brings it all together in a way that is intellectually coherent while meeting the person's spiritual needs. This is a place of rest and of discovery. Because individuals in conjunctive faith are much more comfortable with paradox, they tend to be less threatened by those with different belief systems. A sober person who does not get on his knees to pray every day will not feel as though he is doing something wrong just because a sponsor prays in such a manner. He will know that his relationship with a Higher Power is personal and that he doesn't have to conform to connect. A person in recovery who experienced spiritual bypass in earlier stages of faith development might shed the defense in Stage 5. In addition to having an individual identity in the context of a fellowship, his identity can be both flawed and faultless. In this sense, he might experience Bill Wilson's "design for living that works in rough going."

Stage 6: Universalizing

Stage 6 is simply called universalizing. Fowler describes this stage as involving a "disciplined, activist incarnation—a making real and tangible—of the imperatives of absolute love and justice of which Stage 5 has partial apprehensions." In Stage 6, the ego ceases to be an individual's driving force, and she will willingly give up her possessions, pleasures, even her own life. According to Fowler, examples of people who have reached this stage are Gandhi, Martin Luther King Jr., and Mother Teresa. Although most people will not reach the universalizing stage, it is important to note that reaching Stage 6 does not equal attaining perfection in any sense of the word. One example of someone in the latter stages of faith development who has also experienced spiritual bypass is Ram Dass.

Ram Dass played a pivotal role in bringing Eastern spirituality to Western culture, and he became a great spiritual teacher in the process. In *Spiritual Choices: The Problems of Recognizing Authentic Paths to Inner Transformation,* he has written about his personal experience of being a master teacher on the one hand, while experiencing spiritual bypass on the other.

> What happened was that the spiritual identity played right into my hands psychologically. Psychologically there were whole parts of my being that I was afraid of and didn't accept. I had a justification for getting rid of them by becoming holy, and I was using my spiritual journey psychodynamically in order to get free of things that I couldn't acknowledge in myself. . . . My theory was that if I did my Sadhana hard enough, if I meditated deeply enough, if I opened my heart in devotional practices wide enough, all that unacknowledged stuff would go away. But it didn't.

Ram Dass's story is not only an example of reaching spiritual heights while shrouded in spiritual bypass; it also speaks to the possibility of moving through such an impasse. After ten years on his journey, Ram Dass gained insight into his spiritual development.

> What I experienced was that I had pushed away my humanity to embrace my divinity. . . . Until I could accept my humanity fully, my intuitions weren't going to be fully in harmony with the way of things.
>
> I began to feel that my freedom was going to lie in the creative tension of being able to see simultaneously perfection and also to experience pain; to see that there was nothing to do and yet to work as hard as I could to relieve suffering; to see it was all a dream and still live within the reality of it. My present work is to get into the fullness of the human heart.

Fowler's six stages of faith development and Ram Dass's personal experiences support the idea that, although bypass is not an ideal condition, it may be an inherent part of one's

spiritual journey. M. Scott Peck's model of spiritual development supports the same conclusion, that spiritual bypass may
play a fundamental role in one's spiritual growth.

Peck's Stages of Spiritual Development

Regarding spiritual growth, Peck states in *The Different Drum*
that Fowler is the "most widely read scholar of the subject."
However, Peck created his four stages of spiritual development
based on his own personal and spiritual journey, as well as
through his work as a psychotherapist. Peck's four stages are
chaotic-antisocial, formal-institutional, skeptical-individual, and
mystical-communal.

Stage I: Chaotic-Antisocial

Stage I in this model is called chaotic-antisocial. Peck refers to
this stage as an "undeveloped spirituality." He uses the term
antisocial, because people who fall into this category tend to be
so ego-focused that they do not care about the needs of others.
Many individuals in Stage I will find themselves institutional-
ized; others may be disciplined enough to rise to positions of
great power. I'm sure we can all think of some examples of
people who fit into this category.

In speaking about transitioning from one stage to another,
Peck uses the term *conversion*. "Such conversions are usually
sudden and dramatic and, I believe, God-given," he writes. "It is
as if God had reached down and grabbed that soul and yanked
it up to a quantum leap." This definition of conversion is much
like the one that Bill Wilson experienced and is consistent
with the language of AA. Although a conversion experience is a
transition from one stage to another, Peck also acknowledges
gradations between the stages and provides an example of
someone who goes back and forth between Stages I and II. An
individual in this position is called a backslider. Peck describes
this in detail:

This is the kind of man . . . who drinks, gambles, and leads a generally dissolute existence until some good Stage II folk come along and have a chat with him and he is saved. For the next two years he leads a sober and righteous and Godfearing life until one day he is found back in a bar. . . . He is saved a second time, but once again he backslides, and continues bouncing back and forth between Stage I and Stage II.

Many examples exist of people in recovery who seem to be in this backslider position. They get some time in the program but repeatedly relapse, only to start over once again.

Stage II: Formal-Institutional

Peck calls Stage II of his model formal-institutional. This stage appears to be in alignment with Fowler's Stages 2 and 3. Individuals in Peck's Stage II have very clear boundaries, a sense of right and wrong, and knowledge of what to believe and what not to believe. It is interesting to note that a conversion from Stage I to Stage II can make an individual feel as though he has been saved. This is partly because of the structure he has adopted in place of chaos. To protect this newfound security, people in Stage II often feel threatened if anyone questions their faith. This type of faith almost always includes a vision of God that is external to the individual. As Peck explains, "It is no accident that their vision of God is that of a giant benevolent Cop in the Sky, because that is precisely the kind of God they need." As this stage is similar to Fowler's Stages 2 and 3, it follows that a formal-institutional individual would be a likely candidate for spiritual bypass. For instance, he might adopt very clear rules about recovery to please the benevolent Cop in the Sky, with the understanding that doing so will deliver power and privilege.

Stage III: Skeptical-Individual

Peck's Stage III, skeptical-individual, is very much the same as Fowler's Stage 4. Individuals in Stage III are "active truth seekers."

Peck explains that they have abandoned black-and-white thinking and are "able to get glimpses of the 'big picture' and to see that it is very beautiful indeed . . . and strangely resembles those 'primitive myths and superstitions'" from Stage II. When an individual in Stage III wants to go even deeper in her search for truth, she experiences a conversion to Stage IV.

Stage IV: Mystical-Communal

Stage IV in Peck's model, called mystical-communal, appears to be congruent with Fowler's Stages 5 and 6. "Mystics acknowledge the enormity of the unknown," Peck explains, "but rather than being frightened by it, they seek to penetrate ever deeper into it that they may understand more." Individuals in this stage experience a sense of unity, a perception of "an underlying connectedness between things." As we learned discussing Fowler's model, a person's ability to reach the latter stages of faith development does not make him immune to spiritual bypass. In fact, an argument could be made that greater spiritual pursuits might help to foster bypass, because the more "spiritual" someone becomes, the higher his standards might rise—as was the experience of Ram Dass.

Although Peck outlined four separate stages of spiritual development, he recognized that individuals retain vestiges from previous stages, even as they evolve. By acknowledging this trend toward retention, an individual in Stage IV can recognize that a part of him identifies with the concerns of Stage I. Becoming conscious of this fact allows one to work with the Stage I material. The person can accept his egocentric tendencies and develop ways to work with and through them. He might still feel some shame about his self-centeredness, but he will be able to own it. For example, a person can recognize that he is being dishonest with a sponsor because he doesn't want to look bad in the sponsor's eyes. This recognition might allow the person to tell the sponsor that he is afraid of looking bad, which allows greater discourse and evolution. Peck states, "The beauty of the consciousness that we are all on an ongoing spiritual journey and that there is no end to our conversion" is one of the greatest gifts of spiritual development.

This discussion of the development of faith and spirituality is relevant to our topic of spiritual bypass in recovery because, although the defense can be detrimental, we cannot claim that it is always harmful. Spiritual maturity is just like physical and emotional maturity; it is a process that lasts a lifetime. We have to accept that at any given moment we are somewhere in that ongoing process. We might be brilliantly navigating one area of our life and oblivious in other areas. We might have learned an immense amount about ourselves only to discover facets that we never knew existed. We might be engaged in spiritual bypass at one point and recognize it as bypass only after we have grown out of need to defend that part of ourselves. To identify the impact spiritual bypass may have in our lives, it is useful to understand that bypass does indeed have a softer side, one that doesn't define us as "less than" or "immature," but as mortal and ever evolving.

Growing Pains: Assagioli and Psychosynthesis

Roberto Assagioli was an Italian psychologist who founded a spiritual approach to psychology that he called *psychosynthesis.* His holistic model, explained in Piero Ferrucci's book *What We May Be: Techniques for Psychological and Spiritual Growth Through Psychosynthesis*, includes both the psychological and spiritual realms of development and is therefore an ideal place to further investigate spiritual bypass in the context of healthy psychospiritual development.

Assagioli believed that spiritual development has many inherent gifts, but that it also involves "a necessity for the whole personality to rearrange itself in order to fit the aims and laws" of a larger vision. In the language of AA, *everything* has to change for a person to stay sober and to progress spiritually. Assagioli would agree that development is an ongoing process, but he would extend this thinking to acknowledge that the process is not an easy one. Psychological blocks that have been put in place precisely for protection must be investigated and overcome. Spiritual development, he states, "obliges us to leave our comfort zone, to progress into the unknown, to face the tremendous impact of the Self." This is daunting in and of itself, yet Assagioli acknowledges another challenging aspect of spiritual growth. For many, there is actually a fear of annihilation that occurs in the process of facing who they truly are. What follows is a description of how and why this fear penetrates to the core of an individual:

> There was once a time when each of us met life in an innocent and totally open way, without reservations or defenses. But then something went wrong—our innocence and openness were abused, our love was not returned, our spontaneity was ridiculed, our sensitivity was hurt, or our faith was betrayed. From that time was born a series of reservations and suspicions, ranging from the ordinary common sense of the mature adult all the way to an ingrained resistance, sometimes total, to surrender to the new. One just does not want to be swindled by life again.

For a recovering alcoholic, this description might explain why the person started, or continued, to drink. Alcohol may have been a defense against further wounding. Looking at this in the context of spiritual development, we can see that, to make a full recovery, the alcoholic has to let go of far more than alcohol. This realization makes clear the distinction between becoming dry—which is defined as a cessation of drinking without tending to the underlying causes and conditions for one's drinking—and becoming sober. An alcoholic may have stopped drinking and started to incorporate spiritual principles into her life, but she may not have fully committed to sobriety if it means taking an honest look at her psychological makeup. Just as alcohol was used defensively prior to recovery, other defenses such as spiritual bypass can be operating in one's sobriety. This stepping-stone process can aid a person in facing her fears at a manageable pace. If she had to shed all of her defenses all at once, she would surely return to the safety of the bottle. This is also why many addicts "transfer" addictions when they become sober. The alcoholic starts to use food or starts overspending, overworking, or gambling to numb the pain.

The model of psychosynthesis contains an understanding of the subtle complications that may arise in the process of psychospiritual development. For example, Assagioli spoke to one's survival of wounding, or crisis of transformation, as the precursor to psychospiritual development. He stated, "It is a deeper encounter with the truth of our lives—an encounter that will always shake up the status quo." For an alcoholic, this may be the equivalent of entrance into Alcoholics Anonymous. And for a person in recovery, it may be the continued shedding of defenses as they cease being a protection and start becoming a barrier to greater freedom and consciousness.

In Conclusion

Spiritual bypass clearly has a softer side. The defense mechanism needs to be removed from the stigmatized category in which it often falls and placed in the context of psychospiritual development. Welwood recognized that "using spirituality to make up for failures of individuation [or] psychologically separating from parents" will not cultivate spiritual and psychological health. However, he has witnessed many patients who experienced various forms of spiritual bypass as a transition. In regard to one patient, he stated, "I don't believe his spiritual practice was a failure. It served him well in many ways. It also brought him to the point where his most primitive, unresolved psychological issues were fully exposed and ready to be worked with." From this example, and from the theories of Fowler, Peck, and Assagioli, we can see that spiritual bypass might very well be a necessary transition to a new phase of development in which growth and exploration can begin to be realized.

SEVEN

Chelsea

*"The cave you fear to enter holds
the treasure you seek."*

———— ATTRIBUTED TO JOSEPH CAMPBELL

WHAT FOLLOWS ARE THE HIGHLIGHTS from an interview I conducted with Chelsea. In the interview, we aimed to capture her personal experience of spiritual bypass in recovery. At the time, she was thirty-five years old and had been sober for twelve years.

Chelsea has struggled with issues of abandonment throughout her life. As a young girl, she became very involved in extra-curricular activities in an attempt to feel that she was a part of something. As an adult, she is aware that staying so busy and trying to be a "good girl" were her defenses against having to feel. She believed that if she kept in constant motion, she would not have to acknowledge her painful emotions of anger and loneliness.

When constant activity wasn't enough to protect Chelsea from her feelings, bingeing and purging became her first addiction. Eventually, she discovered drugs and alcohol, and she found that these gave her the greatest sense of relief. Chelsea's defenses of being a good girl, bingeing and purging, and using drugs and alcohol were a prelude to her experiences of spiritual bypass in recovery.

Chelsea grew up Catholic, but she left the religion when she was old enough to determine her own spiritual path and prior to her recovery in AA. She sought congruence between her beliefs and her spiritual practices and realized that she was being hypocritical if she continued in the Catholic faith. After she departed from Catholicism, Chelsea's primary contact with spirituality was the quintessential "foxhole prayer"—asking God for help in a crisis, with a promise to improve her behavior in the future.

When Chelsea hit bottom with drugs and alcohol, she became willing to surrender to a God she didn't truly believe in or understand. She knew that she didn't have the answers to her predicament and believed that surrendering to God was the only alternative to dying an alcoholic death. At some point during this surrender, Chelsea had her first spiritual experience.

AT ONE OF THE LAST JOBS I WALKED OUT ON, this girl I worked with, her name was Erin, and I didn't want to just be friends with her. I kind of wanted to *be* her. She was just like that cool chick, and she had a raspy voice, and she was sober. She had been sober about six or seven months, and she had short punky blond hair and smoked Camel wide cigarettes, and I was like, "God, you are so cool." I had a great time working with her and thought that she was lovely, but at that point in my drinking, if you didn't drink like I did, or at least close to it, I couldn't handle being around you. And at that point I was hanging out with forty- to fifty-year-old men who were stoolies at the local dive bar, because they drank like I did.

So, this time I walked out of my job, Erin took one of the checks that we wrote our orders on and she wrote down her phone number and said, "Call me sometime; I want to know that you are okay." And I threw out the check when I got home, because I was like "There is no way I'm going to call her. She doesn't drink. I have no room for her in my life." And it was really toward the end of my drinking, and I was lying in bed, and

I did Pascal's wager. You know, I was like, "God, I don't know if you exist, but if you do, fucking prove it, or I'm dead. I'm absolutely dead unless you show me that you're here." And I meant it. I knew I was going to die. I was on the doorstep of heroin at that point. And the next morning when I woke up, the check with her phone number on it was on my dresser. I shit you not. And I have no explanation for it, other than that it was a spiritual experience. It was God pointing me in the direction I was supposed to go. I called her, obviously! I called her and she took me to my first meeting.

At my first meeting I cried the entire time. It was the third edition of the Big Book, so it was 1994. October of '94 was when I first started going to AA. And we read the story about the man in the Indian army, whom I had nothing in common with—female, twenty-two years old, in the United States, not in the army, you know—nothing in common with him and I related to every single thing in that story. I cried the entire meeting. I got sober in Milwaukee, and there they have table meetings, so you read as a group and then break up into small groups, and everybody shares. So it is kind of nice because you get to know people and you are in a small group, so you're not as worried about saving face in a smaller group. And I cried the entire time because I knew that was exactly where I needed to be and I hated that. I absolutely hated that I had to go to Alcoholics Anonymous.

In early recovery, Chelsea only worked the first two Steps. She wrestled with her conception of a Higher Power and, therefore, felt that she was unable to take Step Three. Although she had an intellectual understanding of why she needed a Higher Power, she did not have any life experience that would allow her to conceive of a loving relationship with God. She feared true connection and did not want to become vulnerable.

Chelsea was holding on to a sense of control by making sure nobody in AA really knew who she was. She did the bare minimum to stay sober and was still insisting on congruence between her beliefs and her actions. Her inability to close this gap left her unable to "turn her will and life over," and after fourteen months in the program, Chelsea relapsed.

The relapse was premeditated and arose out of a desire to not feel so scared, anxious, and uncomfortable in her own skin. Chelsea was longing to feel better and, although she witnessed other members of AA staying sober and becoming contented in life, she did not feel it was possible for her. She felt unique in her plight and fearful that she would never change, which perpetuated her misery. She believed that if she could not turn her will over to a Higher Power, she would have to take her will back completely.

I WAS SO UNCOMFORTABLE IN MY OWN SKIN. I just felt on edge and prickly and scared all the time. And I was doing euphoric recall, remembering what it was like when I used to drink. But I wasn't going to drink, because in that fourteen months of sobriety I got very, very sick about three months sober.

I had the start of liver damage at age twenty-two and the doctor said to me, "If you drink again, it isn't a question of if you might die; it is a question of when." He said it would be a very short period of time because I was very sick. And that scared me enough, so when I relapsed I actually didn't drink. I smoked pot. And the second I did it, I was like, "What did I do, oh my God, what did I do?" And I'm at home, eating pickles, reading my Big Book, high as a kite, trying to call one person who might remember me from a meeting, because I would come in just as the meeting started and leave the second it ended. I barely shared and I made sure that nobody knew me. I didn't want to be a part of AA. I heard great things, I heard great speakers, I saw other people getting healthy and making friends, and I wasn't having that experience at all. I was absolutely miserable.

But then when I relapsed, I was like, "I don't want this either."
You know, I really surrendered after I relapsed. I was like, I have
to go to AA. And I don't want to, but I have to. And then I was
pissed—really, really angry.

Back in the program, Chelsea recognized that she was angry
with her Higher Power. This was not surprising, because this
defensive posture had always allowed her to feel safe by distancing herself from people who had harmed her. She also saw God
as fallible, which kept her stagnant in recovery for many years.
In hindsight, the one thing Chelsea surrendered by coming back
to AA was the delusion that drinking or using drugs was the
answer to her problems.

To stay sober, Chelsea picked up her old tool of getting
and staying busy, but this time it was recovery-oriented. She
gave "lip service" to Step Three, but she "wasn't feeling what
everybody talked about. I didn't feel that sense of peace and
sense of calm, and I was pissed. I was like 'What is wrong with
me?'" Chelsea dove into service work and working the Steps and
Traditions, which defended her from her feelings and eventually brought her back to the familiar idea that she was incapable
of having a loving experience with God or anyone else. She
longed for these relationships and was angry that she did not
have them.

Eventually, Chelsea "acted as if" she believed in God in
order to continue working the Steps. She did this by believing
that her sponsor believed in her Higher Power, and this third-
party belief was sufficient to get her through the Third Step in a
way that felt acceptable for Chelsea.

While borrowed faith allowed her an initial experience of
all Twelve Steps, Chelsea continued to experience raw emotion
she could not handle. Meetings, sponsorship, and Step work
did not penetrate the level of despair that she felt. She wanted a
new experience, but she did not know how to get it. Chelsea was
suicidal and making a plan to kill herself.

I WAS SUICIDAL AT FOUR AND A HALF, going on five years sober. Nobody really talks about five years sober, but it is awful. I was trying to figure out, all right, how can I do it with the least amount of pain? Pills, well technically wouldn't that be a relapse? [She laughs.] Well, I guess you know everyone says warm water and slitting your wrists, and you know, I was really thinking it through.

And then an old roommate of mine, her sister had a dog, but her fiancé was mistreating him pretty badly. Leaving him in his kennel for twenty hours at a time and hitting him until he would shit himself. It was pretty bad. And she said, "Do you want him?" And I didn't ask my landlady, I just said, "Yes." Because my thinking was, if I got him, I would be less inclined to kill myself, because I lived alone and I wouldn't want the dog to have to eat my hands and feet to survive until they found my body. This was my actual thinking. This was the level of crazy that I was at.

I can look at it now and kind of laugh, but my God, to be in that state where getting a dog was the only way I could save myself. Because I loved animals so much that I wouldn't put an animal through that. And, I mean, I call him my eskimo back into the program, because of the relationship that developed with my dog.

Chelsea's devotion to her dog became her salvation and her reason for living. This relationship also began a process of connection to something outside of herself that she could believe in. After this profound experience, Chelsea began to make some real changes. She asked someone new to be her sponsor, who instructed her to find a Higher Power that was personal to her. She was open to a new experience with God even if she did not believe in Him, and she was dedicated to the ongoing process of discovery.

Discussing Step Three with her new sponsor led to another spiritual experience for Chelsea. She was introduced to the idea that her *conception* of a loving God could *be* her Higher Power.

MY SPONSOR HAD ME WRITE DOWN what my ideal of God was, my ideal Higher Power. And so I'm like, "I'll show you," and I started writing down "unconditional love and open to every type of religious practice, doesn't judge, is there for me in good times and bad" . . . I mean really just laying down what I thought the ideal God was. And a lot of it really had to do with my absentee parents, just that nurturing, caring, loving God that I didn't get growing up, parentalwise.

So I wrote all these things down, went to my sponsor's house, and we sat down and he read it and he said, "Chelsea, you have all this." And it was like a lightbulb just went on. Like, "I have all that! I have all that!" Oh my God, I'm getting teary thinking about it. I have this. It is within me. I mean, then it was like this explosion of . . . God is talking to me through other people, people in my life are teachers that God is sending to me, I mean these are the gifts. I did a 180 about spiritual belief in AA and about God in general. I felt like, "I have had this all along and I chose to turn my back, I chose to be angry, I chose"—and I needed to, because that was what I was doing to survive.

I wasn't self-aware enough yet. I wasn't at that point where I could really say, "There is a loving God in my life." And I didn't even know what to call Him. I often say he looks like Jeff Spicoli from *Fast Times at Ridgemont High,* but with horn-rimmed glasses. You know, kind of doofus-y looking, but really smart. That is my vision of God.

Conceiving of a God who was personal and internal provided a feeling of safety for Chelsea. She could finally let go of the burdens she was carrying, and it became safe to "turn her will and life over." Although this spiritual experience was necessary for Chelsea to move forward in spiritual development, in hindsight, she recognizes that it was also steeped in spiritual bypass.

To avoid having to look at the pain of her past, Chelsea "threw" herself into spiritual practice. She could not get enough of the euphoric feeling she received from spiritual experience, and she sought to intensify it, as if she were seeking the "perfect never-ending high."

I WAS COMPLETELY AVOIDING LOOKING AT ANYTHING having to do with my childhood. It was better to throw myself into meditation, throw myself into prayer, throw myself into looking at different religious beliefs and maybe applying or adopting them. I mean really actively looking for something to fill the God-shaped hole. Because there was a way for me to— I don't have to look at it because I've got God.

It is almost like being a born-again Christian. "I have God, so nothing else matters. It doesn't matter what I did in my past because I'm forgiven; I have God." Well, for me at least, it did matter what happened in my past because I never looked at it. I ignored it. And to have any type of future interacting with people on more than just a superficial level, I have had to look at that. Having God just wasn't quite enough. It definitely felt better than it did before, when I was angry, but that anger was just there. It was almost like alcoholism; it was just sitting there lying dormant.

I didn't even really look at the abuse in my life until the last couple of years. Really took a look at it and really realized that it affected me. It absolutely affected me in every aspect of my life. There was a great deal of physical and emotional abuse in my house growing up. My brother is six and a half years older than I am, and from the time I was eight until I was almost twelve, I was his punching bag. And I had a father who was gone, out of the picture, and a single mom who was a working professional. She did the best she could, also suffering from chronic depression. She just didn't talk, like I was ignored most of the time and really fending for myself. And I couldn't tell anybody this abuse was happening because I didn't feel like anyone had my back. And I am adopted. So automatically underlying all of this is abandonment—father leaves, mother is not present, brother is abusive. So I'm like an after-school special. That is what it feels like sometimes.

This experience typifies the definition of spiritual bypass—using spiritual tools to avoid one's painful emotions—in that Chelsea believed she did not have to address the painful feelings or the truth of her past if she had God in her life.

During her experience with spiritual bypass, Chelsea was completely immersed in AA, making the program her entire life. She did not want to lose her connection with God after so many years spent in turmoil, and anything outside of the fellowship felt threatening. Chelsea became rigid about recovery and judgmental toward others who were not as dedicated to sobriety.

Spiritual striving to overcome her past—while seemingly working a strong program—did not remove Chelsea's anger. Nor did it allow her to move through it. Instead, she channeled her anger through sarcasm. Although she had once felt that she was a nice person, Chelsea no longer believed that about herself. She was full of fear, insecurity, and resentment.

Facing the truth of her circumstances would have meant Chelsea had to accept "life on life's terms." This was not something that interested her. She had an expectation that she would be relieved of unwanted situations and that she was entitled to a life that continually looked and felt better.

I GOT VERY BUSY WITH WORK, very busy with AA, went to a lot of meetings, and when I was about ten years sober, it was like, "Why don't they talk about the ten-year thing? Is this a five-year cyclical thing?" Ten years wasn't as violent as five years—it was more reflective, like "This is what ten years sober feels like and looks like?" I actually shared in a meeting, 'cause the anger bubbled up, the anger took over everything, and I actually said, "If somebody had told me that at ten years sober, this is what it would look like, I wouldn't have quit drinking."

Although spiritual bypass may have looked like a healthy recovery in the context of her peers who were also active in the program, Chelsea's relationship to her Higher Power was an attempt to anesthetize her feelings. The transition from using spirituality to transcend her experience to allowing spirituality to aid her in engaging with her experience was a difficult one.

Chelsea felt self-loathing as she acknowledged the incongruence between her belief system and the way she acted in the world. Her deep faith and desire to amplify her spiritual experience was not evidenced in her relationships. These relationships ultimately became the barometer of her psychological health, and she realized that she could not continue on her same path without risking greater isolation and alienation from her peers.

Chelsea's experience of unintentionally giving spirituality a privileged position over her psychological health was reinforced by much of the direction she received from others in the program, particularly when she became aware of painful feelings and the sole direction she was given was to "pray about it" or "make amends." These solutions were offered frequently, but Chelsea felt that they did not always address or honor her full experience.

People in recovery refer to "outside help" as resources outside the scope of those provided in Twelve Step programs or outside the experiences of its members. When psychological issues arise and they are not recognized as requiring outside help, a sponsor might advise the newcomer to pray or to work the Steps.

Chelsea believes that, in the absence of a reliance on a Higher Power, newcomers often rely on other sober people to provide "good orderly direction" (G.O.D.). This can create a scenario in which newcomers confer a status of Higher Power onto their sponsors. In Chelsea's opinion, prayer can then be interpreted as a "prescription or road map—that this is 'the answer' in AA." Time and experience in the program have allowed Chelsea to understand the dangers in making another human being her Higher Power. Individuals are fallible and their nonprofessional advice can be mistaken for the tenets of AA.

As a sponsor and as a member of many home groups over the years, Chelsea has been witness to others using the "Fake it till you make it" adage as authorization to apply only spiritual principles to their lives, when outside help was ultimately needed. Witnessing this in her peers has reinforced her belief that "acting as if" in a spiritual context is not a cure-all.

Chelsea's experience of spiritual bypass, coupled with the various ways in which she "acted out" with food or sex, kept her abstinent in AA for ten years. She was also able to defend against her anger and trauma throughout this decade of recovery. However, this milestone anniversary began a process of getting honest about the extent of her abandonment, her anger, and her mistrust of others. Her honesty to herself provided the willingness to discuss these issues with another. Although she had participated in therapy in the past, Chelsea had never been entirely truthful or open to the process.

AT TEN YEARS, I WAS DOING A LOT OF WAITING for life to happen to me, like I was waiting for my life to begin instead of living the life I had in front of me. I was very, very depressed and started going to therapy with the therapist I am still with today. And the thing that happened a lot with me in therapy is that I talk a lot, but I don't say a whole lot. I seem very forthcoming, but I'm actually very guarded. I didn't realize that I was that hard to get to know, but I guess I am. I try not to be, but trust isn't exactly something that comes natural to me. It takes a little while for me to build up and really feel like "Okay, I trust you."

I mean, with my therapist, I have been working with him for two years, and finally we are getting to the point where I can say what I need to say. Part of me hates my mom. Part of me hates my family. I don't trust them. And it is very hard to be angry with people who did stuff to you twenty-five years ago when they aren't the same people anymore.

When Chelsea began to face her anger, it no longer had a hold on her. She was able to begin the process of integrating all of her feelings and experiences, so that she could feel less fragmented. This allowed her to build a "right size" sense of self. Although her spiritual awakening at five years of sobriety did include aspects of spiritual bypass, it also began to provide the sense of safety that would enable her to start, five years later, to look at the truth of her emotional wounding.

Currently, Chelsea can tolerate her feelings, knowing that they will pass. She can tolerate her behavior, knowing that she is in the process of growing up. For many years in recovery, Chelsea accepted other AA members' ideas of what it meant to be "sober." She followed conservative rules in the hope they would buy her freedom from her past and from her uncomfortable feelings. She is now recognizing that she has to discover what being sober means to *her* and is practicing the principle of "To thine own self be true."

Chelsea's overreliance on the program and her misconceptions of the virtues of spiritual practice provided a temporary sense of protection. Feeling that she could avoid her unfinished business kept her sober and eventually allowed her the opportunity to go deeper in her recovery. The preparation to go deeper was not premeditated. She did not know what the future would bring, but in retrospect, every aspect of her journey has been necessary to make way for greater spiritual and psychological health. Chelsea's recovery was in God's hands, because, in her own words, "God lays down the road map for me to follow. And then I just have to choose whether or not I'm going to follow it."

WITHOUT HAVING THE SPIRITUAL AWAKENING I had at five years, without having an ongoing spiritual awakening, I would be ill-equipped to deal with what I have been working through. Without faith, I couldn't do the work. You know, it's that whole line of "Faith without work is dead," and I think that it applies to emotional work as much as it applies to Step work or service work or anything else.

It is imperative to me to have a belief in order to go to the dark places that I have had to go. To really look at all of the crap that has happened to me. And really being okay as a result of it. I mean, I'm all right. My spiritual life has allowed me to deal with tragedy. And it's not the chicken or the egg thing. I mean the spiritual awakening had to, for me, it had to come first. I wouldn't have been capable of going any deeper. My faith is like my safety net. It is like I have leapt off of a very high cliff, and I feel like I'm free-falling, but I know there is a net.

Currently, Chelsea attends meetings where there is long-term sobriety. She feels there is a difference between people who are abstinent from drugs and alcohol and people whom she perceives to be sober and serene. In her experience, peace and serenity come from living an examined life. Although it is a blessing not to drink for one day at a time, no matter what the person's psychological condition, Chelsea favors the experience of working on psychological development to gain the most freedom in recovery. Of course, such a statement might also imply that working a program in a "right" way will relieve all suffering—which is another form of spiritual bypass.

Spirituality has become the foundation and the anchor for Chelsea in her efforts to look at her emotional issues. Her faith allows her an intense and intimate experience with her own life. It keeps her safe in the knowledge that she is all right, no matter what is happening. She has finally found peace and freedom by acknowledging her painful past and her emotionally harrowing abandonment experiences. Faith aids Chelsea in acknowledging her fears and in accepting them. This has been one of her recovery's greatest rewards. She comprehends the idea that "This too shall pass" and, even when she doesn't feel that she is being taken care of, Chelsea remembers, "It's just temporary; things are going to work out."

That being said, Chelsea continues to question why life presents her with certain challenges. She questions what "her part" is in relationship to her struggles, with the intention of alleviating future suffering. She retains some residual belief that spiritual practice will remove difficult obstacles. In answer to her question "Why do things keep going wrong?" someone once told Chelsea, "I don't think that God gives us more than we can handle, but I really think that life does." Chelsea agreed and found this to be a profound statement.

Looking back on her recovery, Chelsea understands that staying sober by working the Twelve Steps was just the beginning. She sees that many people in AA stay at this rudimentary level of self-investigation and that it does not yield holistic results. It was by integrating therapy with her AA work that Chelsea found true freedom and self-acceptance. She is aware that there is more work to be done, but she is grateful to be at a place in her recovery where she is comfortable enough to know that she has everything she needs to face the totality of what lies ahead.

PART TWO

EIGHT

There Is No Finish Line

"You cannot step twice into the same river,
for other waters are continually flowing in."

— HERACLITUS

PART TWO OF THIS BOOK will outline the themes discovered in my research on the experience of spiritual bypass by individuals in AA.

My study was the first to explore this topic and the aim was to capture the subjective, or lived, experience of spiritual bypass by people with long-term sobriety. I conducted interviews with people in AA, asking them to provide descriptions of their spiritual and psychological growth and development throughout their recovery. By using a research method called *transcendental phenomenology*, I was able to understand and describe my participants' experiences with bypass in a way that highlighted the building blocks or the essence of the defense mechanism and how it operates. If we wanted to understand the essence of a chair using phenomenology, we might come to understand that despite the many variations that exist in the world, it is inherently seen as something on which we sit. This is a useful example of a theme relating to a chair. The themes related to spiritual bypass similarly reveal various aspects of the defense.

The most prominent theme revealed in my research was that spiritual development in AA is experienced as cyclical rather than linear. Development often begins with an initial surrender to the program or to one's Higher Power, or with a commitment to abstain from drugs or alcohol with or without the intention for spiritual or psychological growth. As a person progresses in recovery, he experiences additional opportunities to surrender, let go, accept, or turn one's will over to a Higher Power. This is sometimes in response to "taking one's will back," discomfort with feelings, a continued obsession with drugs and alcohol, or a tendency to use other things such as money, food, sex, or relationships, to cover up emotional pain. Quite frankly, life is a cause for continual surrender, whether one is in a program or not. Regardless of the impetus, surrender as we've defined it here is never a singular event. It, therefore, needs to be revisited many times in the cause of furthering one's evolution. This cyclical process will continue for as long as the recovering person is participating in a Twelve Step program.

All of the participants in my study expressed a pattern of development that repeatedly cycled through their personal issues. In Allison's story, she described a pattern of vacillating between "surrendering to God and taking her will back." Although the cross on her childhood wall said to "Trust God," she found that she could only trust for so long before she had to pull back. This is not to say that her level of trust didn't grow over the years or that she never went anywhere on her spiritual journey. It is quite the contrary. Allison's path continually led her to more opportunities to "trust." Imagining a life that didn't involve perpetual leaps of faith would probably seem boring to Allison. So she keeps growing and changing, and then getting comfortable and pulling back, which leads to becoming uncomfortable once again, allowing for a new opportunity to surrender.

Cyclical development for Bradford was seen in his lifelong desire to feel "normal," "good enough," or like he wasn't a "fraud." He hoped that the program would relieve him of these feelings but soon recognized that even with sobriety, the feelings remained. So he sought other ways to rise above the human condition, particularly by pursuing spirituality and financial security. Neither of these provided him with the desired goal; however, all of Bradford's pursuits have eventually returned him to a place of surrender. In the process of surrendering, of acceptance and letting go, Bradford ceases trying to overcome himself and learns that he can love himself exactly as he is.

Chelsea's pattern of development has cycled around her fear of abandonment and her hope of becoming "good enough" to be loved and cared for. Both before AA and in recovery, she has tried to distract herself from the painful realities in life by staying really busy. Of course, staying perpetually busy is a method of abandoning herself before anyone else has the chance to do so. The good news is that this tactic never really works. Eventually, Chelsea is forced to face her fears and her reality. Every time this occurs, she finds that she has a greater capacity to see who she is and that she *is* good enough already.

For all of the participants in my study, cyclical development did not mean that there wasn't growth or change over the years or that freedom from certain patterns wasn't achieved. In fact, it is because we are forever moving into different places in our lives that are truly *new* that the pattern itself is not the same as it was experienced before. The fears or anxieties that one experienced before recovery look and feel different when one gets sober. These same issues have a different flavor and influence in a person's twenties than they do in his thirties, forties, fifties, and so on. We are forever discovering nuances that were unavailable to us before. We have a multitude of insights that affect our experience of our patterns. And the patterns are the very things moving us forward, keeping us engaged, and creating the story of our lives.

This theme of cyclical development resonates with physician Charles Whitfield's notion that "what we resist, persists." Although this may seem an ominous warning, the inherent gift in this message is that, if something is not acknowledged or integrated at one stage of life, we will have the opportunity to address it again and again. James Fowler, a minister and professor, was aware that "regression" is a natural transition that enables us to cycle back to previously unincorporated aspects of ourselves so that they may be integrated. The concept of cyclical development, as outlined by both theorists, is certainly evidenced in the experience of people in long-term recovery.

One positive aspect of cyclical development is that there is no finish line in the program and, therefore, no standard of perfection to achieve. No matter how long you stay sober, you will continue to evolve. This attitude can be heard in the AA adage "Progress, not perfection" and in meetings when old-timers speak to the idea that everyone in recovery has only one day of sobriety, the twenty-four hours in which he is currently living.

One way to actively engage in your own cyclical development in the program is to continue working the Steps. Having gone through the Twelve Steps once reveals only what you were conscious of at that time. As the quote at the beginning of this chapter would proffer, we never step into the same river twice. Looking at powerlessness in the first ninety days of recovery is different from looking at powerlessness at five or ten years of recovery. What a person recalls in his first Fourth Step inventory —perhaps before marriage, or the new job, or the loss of a parent, etc.—cannot act as a blanket inventory for the rest of his journey. Just as prayer and meditation are daily practices that evolve and change over time, so too are the rest of the Steps.

Some people have a commitment to work all Twelve Steps every year. Others, like Allison and Chelsea, find themselves as newcomers in a different Twelve Step program once they have some recovery in their original program. A client of mine once said, "Most people don't obtain real emotional sobriety until they have recovery in at least two other programs." People who find themselves in need of more than one program may initially resent the fact that they have to attend more meetings. However, most people eventually come to feel "freedom from the bondage of self" once they surrender the way they think it should be for a way that actually works.

Another client of mine, Denise, recalls going through the Steps for a second time when she was five years sober. She had a new sponsor who wanted to start at Step One to establish the new sponsor/sponsee relationship. One day Denise was complaining to her sponsor about all of the things that were not going well in her life. She was about to lose her job, her boyfriend had broken up with her, and she was afraid that she could no longer afford her home. Denise was angry that recovery had not yielded her a more stable, fulfilling life. She looked around at meetings and saw other women in recovery who had wedding rings on their fingers, enjoyed a host of friends, and went on extravagant vacations. Denise felt as though she were being left behind. She had worked as good a program as any of these other women, so why was she not getting the same results?

Denise's sponsor, Laura, invited Denise to read the Big Book out loud together. Laura could see that Denise had lost sight of where she had come from and all of the gifts that she *did* have in her life. Denise was clearly experiencing spiritual bypass in her thinking that staying sober in AA would deliver every dream that she had for herself. The pair took turns reading one paragraph at a time; they would stop along the way to reflect on what stood out in the reading and to have a brief discussion on that section.

At some point during the reading, Denise started to cry. She was overcome with gratitude for the fact that she was an alcoholic who had not had a drink for more than five years. Denise came from a long line of alcoholics and was the first in her family to get sober. Upon realizing the enormity of this fact, she was relieved of her anger and fear about what she didn't have. Revisiting her powerlessness to stop drinking, in the context of her current sobriety, was such a miracle that she felt ashamed for thinking that the program should have given her more. If Denise hadn't been working with her sponsor, she may have missed this opportunity for profound spiritual growth and renewed gratitude for her recovery.

It is important to remember that working the Steps in this context appears to provide an example of adaptive bypass— a fluid, flexible experience that did not preclude further growth and development for Denise. As mentioned previously, it is not the action or idea that defines something as helpful or harmful. It is the underlying drive and outcome. Denise was able to move through her bypass—her expectation that AA would make all of her dreams come true—by continuing to work the Steps. For another AA member, continually working the Steps could be a form of maladaptive bypass if he were forever trying to avoid the truth of who he is and his present circumstances.

Another adaptive use of revisiting the Steps is that the journey can provide an opportunity to redefine one's conception of a Higher Power. One of the great gifts of Twelve Step programs is the ability to establish your own conception of a Higher Power. The longer you are sober, the more you might seek to establish a new conception. What worked for you in early recovery may not be what works for you to stay sober or to be comfortable in your sobriety. As one's life progresses, it stands to reason that sobriety would need to shift to accommodate the growth.

For some, the word *God* was useful at the beginning of recovery. It felt like a "great power," and after all, the word is used in all of the prayers recited at meetings. This universal vocabulary made it easy to talk with others about spirituality and it increased a sense of connection. But at some point, the word *God* can start to feel limiting or rigid. Despite the power and influence it carries, the word can also come with the notion of a man in the sky. This idea of "God" might not be a personal one, which means the language is getting in the way of the aspiration for "conscious contact." So one might experience periods of nonbelief or cycle back through the Steps from a platform of sobriety to come up with a new conception of a Higher Power. Of course, this is only one example of revisiting the language of and relationship to one's Higher Power. This process unfolds in as many ways as there are people in the program.

People often talk about recovery as an onion, with one layer at a time peeled back. At the end of the day, we are still dealing with an onion. The layers do not suddenly reveal a shiny red fire truck. Spiritual bypass may create an expectation that the onion becomes something other than itself, but honoring recovery as a cyclical process will usually take someone back to gratitude for his onion roots. In this context, I want to remind the reader that cyclical development does not mean one needs to constantly run around in circles to progress. Although I have highlighted ways that people can actively engage in their sobriety, "More will be revealed" is a signal that we can trust the process of recovery. Although surrender is not a singular event, it is not something to be constantly on the lookout for. Working the Steps and reenvisioning one's Higher Power are ways that a person can adaptively progress—but they can also be methods for escaping the present via spiritual bypass. Only you can know when and how you are using the tools to good purpose, and in the end, even if you miss a potential cue for greater consciousness, you will surely have another opportunity down the road.

NINE

Lost in Translation

"In the early days of A.A. I spent a lot of time trying to get people to agree with me, to practice A.A. principles as I did, and so forth. For so long as I did this . . . A.A. grew very slowly."

— BILL W.

LITERAL INTERPRETATIONS OF AA LITERATURE, spiritual practices or principles, or another's conception of what it means to work the program are often used at some point during one's recovery. Although such understanding can become an entry point to more personal and profound conceptions, conversely it can cloud a person's ability to discover what the texts, principles, or practices in the program intimately mean. This can inadvertently lead to spiritual bypass. Literal conceptions ultimately need to be investigated to digest and comprehend what is most relevant and meaningful to each individual. When this occurs, the AA adage "To thine own self be true" can be internalized.

It's in Black and White

After seventy years and four editions, the basic text of *Alcoholics Anonymous*, affectionately known by AA members as the Big Book, has received very few amendments. An attempt to preserve what recovering individuals often refer to as "divinely inspired" material has maintained verbiage that can be construed as inconsistent with the program's goal of spiritual recovery. In part one, we covered some examples of this phenomenon, such as interpreting The Promises that "always materialize" to mean that a person's feelings of pain, confusion, or sadness are indicators that she is doing something "wrong." Just as some religious texts lose their poignant symbolism when interpreted literally, it stands to reason that the immortal words of AA's co-founder have been similarly canonized. To tease out phrases from the Big Book and conclude they are gospel is a shortsighted view of a much bigger spiritual picture.

When individuals in recovery interpret the Big Book literally, it can become a vehicle to judge themselves and others. This was the case with Bradford. When he read the book as specific directions, it allowed him to defend against his vulnerability by believing there was one precise way of achieving all of his goals. If he followed strict instructions, he could finally feel "normal" and would transcend all of his difficulties. This belief system also had him viewing other members of the program as lazy or unwilling if they were not following the same rigid rules.

Many people in the program participate in meetings designed specifically to study the literature. These meetings are called Big Book studies and Step studies. Often a dictionary is used to define certain words in an attempt to figure out exactly what the authors were trying to say. The idea is that the founders were enlightened about the topic, and if a person follows their path as closely as possible, he will be more likely to remain sober. Some go so far as to study the Oxford Group, a Christian organization that influenced Bill Wilson a great deal, or the original Twelve Steps, which contain a slight variation on the current wording. These can be useful and enlightening exercises; however, they can also be used against the person, as we learned in Bradford's story. Bradford's conviction that he was intrinsically "not good enough" prior to recovery was only perpetuated by finding a measuring stick in the program to show how he was still falling short.

Practices and Principles

Literal interpretations of the program's spiritual practices or principles can create a barrier to personal growth and development. For example, prayer can be appropriated by a person's inner-addict as a method for acquiring what she wants or for instant gratification. We saw examples of this in Allison's belief that praying for the diamond ring made it so and in Bradford's theory of prayer as a tool for acquisition. How many times have you heard someone talk about praying for a parking spot just before they turned the corner and found an available space? Of course we love these stories, but what happens when we don't get what we ask for? What happens when the ring isn't delivered, the parking space doesn't appear, or in the larger scheme of things, when our loved one's health doesn't improve? Does this mean that prayer doesn't work? When viewed literally as "ask and you shall receive," prayer can feel more punitive than supportive if it doesn't provide what we are longing for. This can send a person ever deeper into self-doubt and loneliness because the God of his understanding isn't "listening."

The same is true for the practices of meditation or chanting. A person can sit and meditate on an issue in the hope that the issue will be resolved. Chanting is a more active practice that can be employed for the same purpose. Just as with prayer, meditation or chanting can be used defensively in the service of bypassing underlying painful feelings. For this reason, it is important to ask yourself whether you are using these practices to check *in* or to check *out*. Prayer, meditation, and chanting can be extraordinary practices that support a person in the context of the human condition, while making more space for one to feel and access his experiences. However, when these practices are used to check out from life, someone can actually resemble what he looked like when he was still using drugs or alcohol. He does not have more space to access his feelings because his practices are in service of deflection and denial. He is therefore not much better equipped to show up for "life on life's terms."

When it comes to using the program's principles defensively, I want to tell you about a man named Eddie who came to me for therapy. He was very proud of having long-term recovery in Narcotics Anonymous (NA), but he felt as though he was still running from something. It became quickly evident that Eddie took the program's three legacies of recovery, unity, and service very seriously. He was diligent about service in particular and felt it gave him the sense of belonging that he had always wanted. In addition to having several service commitments at meetings, such as making the coffee and being a greeter, he often had ten or more sponsees at one time and spoke on many panels that brought meetings into prisons and institutions.

While Eddie consciously believed that he was working a strong program, it wasn't until he came to therapy that he realized he was doing so much service out of fear. He was afraid that his worth was determined by his altruism and that he would never make up for all he had done while he was still using drugs and alcohol. Because of this, Eddie could not feel or integrate the love he was receiving in his life. His need to feel a part of something and to have a sense of belonging was not truly being satisfied. If he believed the only reason he belonged was because he worked so hard, he didn't really belong at all.

Eventually, Eddie realized that he had to stop bypassing his feelings of insecurity. We were able to face and care for his woundedness, which enabled him to pull back on all of the service he was doing. When he stopped being so busy, he could begin to face his demons and to have compassion for himself in the process. This allowed him to start integrating his altruistic side with his wounded side, without feeling like either aspect completely defined him as a man. From this fuller experience of himself, he could begin to take in the love and gratitude that surrounded him.

Eddie's experience of moving through spiritual bypass, as it related to the principles of the program, echoed throughout Chelsea's story. Chelsea believed that if she could be a "good girl," she would be loved and accepted. She also thought her goodness would allow her to escape her painful feelings. People who are experiencing spiritual bypass often avoid their psychological frailties by engaging in compulsive caring for others; this behavior is frequently born out of low self-esteem and a desire for acceptance. As we have discussed, service commitments and sponsorship are healthy aspects of recovery, but when used defensively, someone might lose sight of her own recovery by putting everyone else's needs before her own. In this case, the service is more a product of shame than of social conscience.

The program's adage "Progress, not perfection" seems to be inverted in all of these examples. Perfectionism occurs when someone cannot tolerate anything less than excellence for fear he will be seen as pathetic. In a positive sense, perfectionism can drive people to do great things, ever striving for the next rung on the ladder. However, it can also become a debilitating condition, creating tremendous amounts of anxiety in a person. A perfectionist in the program will always be striving to improve and cannot tolerate any shortcomings or difficulties. He might believe, "If only I were more willing, humble, honest, or courageous . . . then I'd be okay." Every principle of the program becomes an opportunity to be "better," with an expectation that *this time* he will overcome his low self-esteem. When someone is engaged in this type of thinking, he has no room to be afraid, vulnerable, or existing in the unknown. He sees such experiences as indicators that he is not being willing, humble, honest, or courageous *enough*. It is possible that being unable to recognize or own one's difficulties could be a prelude to relapse, if a person eventually gives up perfection for the relief that could only be found in his drug of choice.

The Borrowed Path

Some sponsors have adopted rules that their sponsees must follow if they are going to work together. Such rules can be very containing for both parties, as each individual knows what to expect from the other and what they each need to do to stay sober. Some of the rules that sponsors prescribe are as follows: go to ninety meetings in ninety days, call your sponsor every day, get a service commitment, call at least three other alcoholics every day, read "On Awakening" from *Alcoholics Anonymous* on page 86 every morning, say the Third and Seventh Step prayers every morning, always know what Step you are working on, etc. These rules are not written in any of the literature but are a compilation of ways that people have worked the program that have been passed down through the collective conscious of Twelve Step recovery throughout the decades.

If a sponsee takes these rules to be literal prescriptions for how to work a successful long-term program, she might become overwhelmed. She might find it difficult to discover how many meetings she needs or wants to regularly attend, what prayers or spiritual practices most resonate, or what sort of service she is suited to carry out. In second-stage recovery, when a person has a good foundation of sobriety and is working on maintaining her program, being able to answer these questions becomes integral to the process.

In some Twelve Step programs, such as Overeaters Anonymous (OA), Debtors Anonymous (DA), and Al-Anon, the flexibility to define what recovery means to each individual is built into the program. By this I mean that *abstinence* is not clearly defined when you walk in the door. In AA, abstinence means refraining from drinking one day at a time. In OA, abstinence cannot mean refraining from eating one day at a time. People in OA say they have to take their disease out for a walk several times a day and then lock it up in between meals. Some members of OA are overeaters and some are undereaters. Some purge their calories by vomiting, some purge by overexercising, and others never purge at all. For these reasons, defining abstinence is a very personal process. A newcomer can borrow ideas from others in the program, but in the end, she is responsible for knowing what does and does not trigger her food and body obsession.

The same is true of DA in terms of defining a personal plan for recovery. DA comprises a wide range of people who have different issues with money. Some are underearners and some earn a great deal but compulsively spend every penny. Earning a particular amount of money, or spending a particular amount of money, cannot concretely define recovery. It is a personal process of discovery related to gaining clarity about a person's finances, his relationship to money, and his self-worth.

Al-Anon is another program in which living in the gray is built into the program's philosophy. One person's boundary is another person's comfort zone. All of these programs offer useful examples of how a person may be forever dealing with his "isms," but can always find personal, authentic ways in which to live comfortably.

In Conclusion

Literal interpretations of literature, spiritual practices or principles, or another's conception of recovery can lead to spiritual bypass. Although people have a tendency to seek an ultimate path to find the ultimate truth, it is when someone investigates what truth means to himself that real meaning is cultivated.

It is important to remember that I am only referencing the ways in which people might misuse the tools of the program so that you can make the distinction of how to use them to good purpose. I am not offering the shadow side of the story to act as yet another measuring stick of how to do it "right" or "wrong." The point is to offer all of the colors on the palette so you can decide how you want to paint them together into your own unique portrait of spirituality and recovery. I hope you will give yourself permission to ask whether following specific directions feels like a good fit or whether praying for a particular outcome feels helpful. There are certainly times when these are useful practices. Prayer, meditation, reading the literature, and practicing spiritual principles are all wonderful tools. The goal here is to enable more consciousness about what you are doing and why you are doing it.

TEN

In My
Defense

"If you hate a person, you hate something in him that is a part of yourself. What isn't part of ourselves doesn't disturb us."

—— HERMANN HESSE,
DEMIAN, THE STORY OF EMIL SINCLAIR'S YOUTH

HAVING LEARNED A LOT about spiritual bypass, we are now aware that defense mechanisms are unconscious strategies we use to protect ourselves from unwanted feelings and painful realities. It is not uncommon for different defense mechanisms to exist simultaneously. For instance, if I am in denial, unable to cope with reality, the chances are good that I am also engaged in another defense such as rationalization, convincing myself of my perceived reality. After I analyzed my research participants' experiences of spiritual bypass, it became clear that in addition to bypass, they also had experienced other defenses, such as projection, introjection, and conflation.

Projection

Projection occurs when you ascribe your unwanted thoughts, feelings, or behaviors onto another. For example, if you are feeling guilty for stealing something, you might be suspicious that people are stealing from you. The same can be true of positive qualities we hold. Perhaps you are not able to own or identify your intelligence, but you can readily see it in others. There is a saying in AA that can help you discern when you are projecting something onto someone else: "If you spot it, you got it."

The research on spiritual bypass revealed that project-ing human attributes onto God, such as being judgmental or fallible, is a common theme in recovery. This defense serves to protect us from our fear of being hurt and is especially common if a person has a history of being abused or neglected. I have witnessed this phenomenon many times in my clinical work. A person's original concept of a Higher Power was his parent(s) or caregiver(s), so the person has a natural tendency to project the features of this primary relationship onto God. If a parent was punishing or unavailable, it is hard to understand how a relationship with God would be any different. Conceiving of a loving Higher Power if a person has never felt truly loved can feel like an impossible task. It is easier for that person to fit God into his current paradigm of having to fend for himself than to risk being let down yet again. Roberto Assagioli, the Italian psychologist who founded psychosynthesis, expressed this sentiment when he talked about the fear of annihilation and wrote, "One just does not want to be swindled by life again."

Despite having a belief that a supportive and loving God exists, resisting practices that could bring conscious contact with one's Higher Power is an example of a person projecting her inability to trust onto God. The person knows intellectually that prayer and meditation are powerful tools, but the underly-ing feeling she has when involved in such practices is that she is putting her dysfunction in the spotlight—to be evaluated and ridiculed. She does not feel as though she is being seen in a loving, compassionate way but rather as though she is being caught red-handed for the imperfect person she is. She cannot trust that God will love her unconditionally. Thus, the conscious contact does not grow, and the inability to trust is amplified. Growing up in an environment in which you couldn't trust your caretakers to "have your back" can make it extremely difficult to experience a loving Higher Power in recovery. You have to become vulnerable to dismantle the projection and to build an experience of trust and connection to something Greater.

We saw an example of this in Chelsea's story. She had an intellectual understanding of why she needed a Higher Power, but her history of abuse did not allow her to believe she could have a loving relationship with God. She ultimately feared true connection and did not want to become vulnerable to anyone or anything. As a way of distancing herself from the possibility of pain, Chelsea was angry with God. He was responsible for all of the harm she had encountered in her life, and thus He was clearly fallible and could not be trusted.

This belief system kept Chelsea stuck in her recovery for many years. She remained in a tremendous amount of pain and had no idea how to handle it. Eventually she became suicidal, which brought her to a "do or die" place of surrender. Before she was able to take her own life, she realized she was the sole caretaker for the dog she had recently adopted. Recognizing this bond was a powerful example of a true connection to something outside of herself. This spiritual experience propelled Chelsea out of her angry projections onto God and into a new phase of her recovery. Her story is a wonderful example of how someone can start with a seeming inability to connect with a Higher Power but, through amplifying even the smallest examples of connection in life, can build a robust foundation of faith.

Another method for finding a faith that works can be seen when we look at the positive benefits of projection. Perhaps you have no experience of love, support, or nurturance, but you want to build these aspects into a relationship with a Higher Power. Such attributes can be projected onto God to create an opening for a relationship unlike any other. In this way, projection can be a useful tool to create the Higher Power you have always wanted. This has been a means of working Step Two in the program for many years.

People have come up with many ways to use the positive aspects of projection. For example, you may want to write a "want ad," looking for a new Higher Power. Or you may design a wish list with the explicit instruction that you are to dream big and not restrict any of what you wish for, even if you think it is impossible. An example of such a wish list or want ad might read like this:

HIGHER POWER WANTED

Must meet *all* of the following criteria:
- Be much more powerful than my disease.
- Be available 24 hours a day, 7 days a week.
- Have my best interests in mind, even when I do not.
- Love me unconditionally, even when I do not know what that means.
- Never "teach me a lesson," but support me through whatever life brings my way.
- Be my biggest cheerleader.
- Give me a shoulder to cry on.
- Have a great sense of humor.
- Be so accessible that I feel you as a part of me.
- Give me the courage and strength to show up for life on life's terms.

When you have come up with your own list, you can choose to believe that your Higher Power already fulfills these criteria. Chelsea did this when her sponsor told her that her conception of a Higher Power *was* her Higher Power. Bill Wilson had this experience when it was suggested that he could choose his own conception of a Higher Power. In "Bill's Story" in *Alcoholics Anonymous* he states,

That statement hit me hard. It melted the icy intellectual mountain in whose shadow I had lived and shivered many years. I stood in the sunlight at last.

It was only a matter of being willing to believe in a Power greater than myself. Nothing more was required of me to make

my beginning. I saw that growth could start from that point. Upon a foundation of complete willingness I might build what I saw in my friend. Would I have it? Of course I would!

Thus was I convinced that God is concerned with us humans when we want Him enough. At long last I saw, I felt, I believed.

The difference between unconscious projections of things that do not serve and conscious projections of things that do can be quite vast. I hope our brief review of this topic can be a useful point of reference in your own recovery.

Introjection

Introjection happens when you take unwarranted responsibility for external traits, concepts, or outcomes and internalize them as your own. For example, if your parents often made you feel guilty, you might internalize that you are a guilty person. Even in the absence of any guilty behavior, you have introjected guilt as a fixed aspect of your being. In a positive sense, introjection might allow you to internalize a good work ethic or the idea that you are kind and compassionate.

Bradford's story revealed his tendency to introject the power of spiritual practices. At one point in his sobriety, he believed that he had the power to create a life beyond his wildest dreams if only he prayed for it. He wanted to stay in control, so he found spiritual methods and ideas that fit with his desire to be in the driver's seat of recovery. Ultimately, this was not a foolproof conceptualization, because he was not able to pray his way to permanent freedom and financial wealth. It was through confronting his darkest truths and experiences, not in overcoming them, that Bradford was able to have conscious contact with God. He wanted to believe he had the power to overcome the human condition, but real power came from recognizing that darkness and light are two sides of the same coin. Owning the darker aspects of life, such as uncomfortable feelings, fear, and vulnerability, allowed him to really own the lighter aspects of himself, including creativity, intelligence, and connection to others.

Every Twelve Step program is filled with examples of people who have fallen into introjection and consequently fallen into relapse. Many feel as though they have learned enough, owned enough, or become powerful enough to start drinking or using in safety again. Fortunately, some come back to the program to share that the disease is progressive and that, when they stopped working a program, they fell back into active addiction. Others are not so fortunate to come back and tell the tale. Some people feel too ashamed to admit that their defenses led to relapse, and others never regain the desire to seek recovery at all.

Conflation

Conflation occurs when two or more things that share some of the same characteristics become confused so there appears to be one single identity. It is basically a fusion or amalgamation. Fusing spirituality, either with materialism or with the notion that a person should not have to assume responsibility for his psychological fitness, is a potential pitfall in recovery. Spiritual bypass is increasingly more likely when these conflations occur. In both cases, spiritual growth can be mistaken for a perceived status of perfection through the absence of either material struggles or emotional difficulties. To progress both spiritually and psychologically, the addict must recognize and deconstruct the conflation.

Conflating spirituality with materialism results in spiritual materialism. As described in chapter two, Chögyam Trungpa defines spiritual materialism as "deceiv[ing] ourselves into thinking we are developing spiritually when instead we are strengthening our egocentricity through spiritual techniques." Regarding manifesting material wealth in a spiritual manner, author and spiritual teacher Michael Beckwith writes in *Spiritual Liberation,*

Many people write to me asking what they're doing wrong when the law of manifestation doesn't deliver their desired style of life. . . . The universe is not concerned with whether or not we have the top ten symbols that announce to ourselves and to the world that we have "made it." This type of material achievement is not the sign of our spiritual attainment.

Allison confused the diamond ring that her husband bought for her as an example of a spiritual reward. In reality, her newfound sobriety and spiritual path were separate from her relationship with her husband, her desire for him to buy her the jewelry, and his ability to purchase it.

Bradford consciously sought a path to spirituality that would afford him success and wealth. He eventually found a religion that supported this goal, but he was unaware that this process led to perpetuating his spiritual materialism. Such materialism has the potential to devalue the importance of a Higher Power and to inflate the importance of one's influence over a desired outcome. As Bradford put it, "The evidence of my spirituality was my manifestation of material things." Although this conflation allowed him to long for "something more," the goals were only on the material plane. The only way to pursue spiritual development, therefore, was to acquire more wealth. This led to detrimentally grandiose financial decisions and an inflated sense of self that had Bradford thinking he no longer needed AA.

Spirituality can often be conflated by individuals in recovery with the notion that they do not need to work on themselves outside of their spiritual practice. Since the literature says that working a spiritual program would "solve all my problems," one can be resistant to any sort of outside help. Some people in the program are leery of therapy because they had seen a therapist for years before they got sober and the therapist could never relieve them of their alcoholism. Of course, no human power can cure addiction. However, once an individual becomes sober, psychological issues may not be addressed by working the Twelve Steps and other helpful resources can be sought. One such example follows.

Jennifer was resistant to therapy for many years after she got sober. In fact, once she was in AA, she felt that going back to therapy meant that she was "sicker" than other members of the program. This idea solidified her low self-esteem, and she came into therapy feeling very defeated. However, in coming to see me, Jennifer challenged her idea that spirituality should in fact remove her emotional issues, and she became open and available to meeting her needs in ways the program couldn't offer. Because a therapist is trained in ways that a sponsor or peer generally is not, therapy can be an excellent adjunct for health and wellness. It is unfortunate that some people in the program feel they are doing something wrong if they need or even want access to different therapeutic modalities.

To take the idea a bit further that a person's spirituality can be conflated, he might actually consider his sobriety as a "get out of jail free" card. If sobriety is fused with personal responsibility, he might use the fact that he is sober to relieve himself of being responsible for anything other than not drinking. For instance, Mike was a client of mine who believed that his wife should just be grateful that he was sober and that she shouldn't be nitpicky about household or familial responsibilities. He acted as though his sobriety should pacify everyone who wanted more from him. In reality, a recovering person does not get a free pass just because he is in recovery. Although some people do need to take things slowly as they become acquainted with a sober life, playing the "sober card" as though they are too fragile to show up for life is not the kind of emotional sobriety that is encouraged in the program.

This same idea can be applied in the context of personal powerlessness. One can conflate being powerless over her addiction with powerlessness to show up for her recovery. Recognizing powerlessness over drinking is not a loophole for avoiding recovery. It is often said that AA is a program for people who want it, not for people who need it—which is to say that a person must be willing to do what it takes to achieve sobriety. Clearly, claiming powerlessness does not absolve anyone from her responsibilities, and such a conflation will most likely need to be teased apart for her to obtain sobriety in AA.

All these conflations can become sticky places where people can get off track in recovery or possibly set themselves up for relapse. Spirituality is an opportunity to connect with our spiritual nature. It is not a panacea that promises to connect us with material wealth or psychological health. It is not a badge of honor that absolves personal responsibility or opportunities for growth. There is nothing wrong with pursuing material wealth, but Bradford's story is a welcome reminder that if spirituality is conflated with materialism, we are really left in a bind when the money stops flowing. The same is true when it comes to our emotional well-being. Just as spiritual fitness doesn't render us physically fit, neither does it render us psychologically healthy. We are made up of mind, body, and spirit, interconnected aspects of the human condition that cannot be simply fused.

ELEVEN

My Way or the Highway

"Your vision will become clear only when you look into your heart. Who looks outside, dreams. Who looks inside, awakens."

— CARL JUNG

PEOPLE IN RECOVERY ARE OFTEN DETERMINED to hold on to a sense of control. Because we can never really control our feelings, other people, or the results from our actions, these control-seeking behaviors are not actually in the service of "control" but of spiritual bypass. Such behaviors include taking contrary action with the expectation of yielding certain results, using unconscious manipulation, engaging in magical thinking, using tools of recovery to maintain a self-centered stance, and remaining isolated.

Contrary Action

As referenced in Allison's story, recovering alcoholics can misinterpret the principle of taking contrary action to mean that *any* contrary action will produce a favored outcome. Contrary action, as defined in *Alcoholics Anonymous*, is based on the idea that "all of A.A.'s Twelve Steps ask us to go contrary to our natural desires." One example of applying this principle in its intended form is when a person doesn't want to show up for a job interview out of fear that he won't be good enough, but he "suits up and shows up" anyway.

Misguided applications of contrary action maintain the illusion that someone can control and manipulate his life. This false sense of power feels good when the results are positive, such as when it results in acquiring an object of affection. However, the shadow to such a belief system is that all actions become an opportunity to manifest either a positive or negative result. This places an unnecessary and inappropriate amount of pressure on the recovering individual. We saw an example of this when Allison believed that not getting on her knees to pray actually created her deep depression.

One way to discern whether you are using contrary action as a method for control or for getting out of your own way is to simultaneously apply the AA tool of "Taking the action and letting go of the results." If you are not in the "results business," you are much less likely to bypass your feelings by taking contrary action.

Unconscious Manipulation

Unconscious manipulation is a potential pitfall in recovery. It is unconscious because the person is not aware of the attempt to influence or control a particular situation at the time. We saw examples of this when Chelsea tried to manipulate God through her foxhole prayers—telling Him that if He does this, then she'll do that. Later in sobriety, she used her relationship with God as an attempt to anesthetize her feelings altogether. As we will see in the following story, people can use the Steps as a way of unconsciously influencing others for their own personal gain.

Frieda had been sober for eight months when she began her amends process in Step Nine: "Made direct amends to such people wherever possible, except when to do so would injure them or others." Many of her initial amends were general in nature, because she was apologizing for being "selfish, [for being] dishonest, and for embarrassing people." In a sentence, she was "sorry for being such a drunk lush."

One of the amends Frieda made during this time was to her former fiancé, Jake. During the amends, she told him that she was in AA working the Steps and that she was striving for a better life than she had previously lived. The amends went well and Frieda continued to stay in touch with Jake for the next three years.

Although Jake was dating other women, Frieda began to realize that her phone calls to Jake were an effort to make sure that he still had affection for her. She would be flirtatious on the phone, they would recall fun times from the past, and the connection would be reestablished. This went on until Frieda was almost four years sober.

Just before her fourth anniversary in AA, Frieda quit smoking cigarettes. The emotions that surfaced during this time were overwhelming and, in her own words, "I fell apart." She was longing to be comforted and, although she was dating someone at the time, he was unaffectionate toward her. She didn't have the courage to ask for her needs to be met in this new relationship, so she retreated to where she had last received real affection. She turned her attention back to Jake.

Frieda's thoughts of her ex-fiancé had her recall when the two had become pregnant many years ago. She knew at the time that she was drinking too heavily to carry the pregnancy and that she would not be the kind of mother she would like to be one day. She immediately made up her mind about having an abortion. When she told Jake that she was pregnant, she simply said, "I've got a bun in the oven, but don't worry about it. I have a doctor's appointment and everything is taken care of. I just need you to drive me there, because they don't want me to drive home afterward."

Jake asked her if she wanted to talk about the possibility of keeping the baby, but Frieda didn't budge. Jake took her to the appointment, and they never talked about the pregnancy again. Although Frieda had done some emotional healing around the abortion when she got sober, she realized that she had never made an amends to Jake for the way she handled everything.

She consulted with her sponsor about this and asked, "Do people ever go back and do 'advanced amends'?"

Frieda expressed all of the reasons that she felt bad about how she had managed her decisions around the abortion. She had never given Jake an opportunity to have his own experience or opinion. Frieda's sponsor advised that only Frieda could know for sure, but that it sounded as though it felt important for her to make an amends and that she should go ahead.

In retrospect, Frieda realizes that she did not discuss with her sponsor how lonely she was feeling or how she was longing for the sort of connection that she once had with Jake. In her heart, Frieda knew what she really wanted from this amends process was to hear that Jake still loved her. She wanted to reestablish the safety net she had once felt with him and to know that he still cared. She didn't want to be with him, but she wanted to be wanted.

Frieda called Jake. She expressed her heartfelt amends, and he responded that it had all happened so long ago and that he held no ill will. He told Frieda that he wished he knew her better now because she sounded like she had become a really great person. He also told Frieda that he was engaged to a woman who was very patient and kind and that he was very happy.

Frieda's heartbreak was overwhelming. She was embarrassed that she had opened her mouth. She immediately saw that the amends had not been about justice; it had been about creating drama to pull Jake's attention back to her. She took a sensitive topic and used it for her own benefit. It was manipulative to misuse something so personal, all in the name of the Ninth Step and The Promises.

In hindsight, Frieda would have left this topic alone. Her motives were to hear Jake say that he missed her. Not only did he *not* say what she wanted; he also expressed surprise to hear that she still went to AA meetings. This made Frieda feel terrible. She didn't look desirable, and she felt pathetic. She had been so sure Jake would make her feel better, but the conversation made her feel much worse.

After her embarrassment and anger subsided, Frieda was able to take a step back and gain a fresh perspective. She reflected on how much she has gained by being in AA and admitted to herself that she does need continuous meetings and that there is nothing wrong with that. She realized through this gut-wrenching experience just how confused she had been about the idea that "God works through other people." She had originally taken this to mean she needed to go to other people for her needs to be met. She came to realize that if God works through people, He could work through her as well. God could work through her and for her, even through the difficult emotional experiences she was having.

Since this time, Frieda has slowly learned to love herself like she never had before. This started with basic things like taking better care of herself. She reached out and started therapy and recognized how much she needed to grieve over her relationship with Jake. She traveled abroad in an effort to connect with her spiritual path. Through both of these endeavors, Frieda moved her attention from the external, that is, other people, to the internal, her emotions and her instincts, which provided an ever-present relationship to God. She came to know the importance of "home" by connecting to herself in ways she had never experienced.

Frieda knows that the majority of the first amends that she made were not necessary. She lived in a small town and many people knew she went to rehab. Making amends was her way of showing everyone how great she looked and how well she was doing. At the time, Frieda had thought that she had infringed on other people's lives when she was drinking, but she now knows that this really wasn't the case.

Today, Frieda takes amends very seriously, both for herself and for her sponsees. She pays special attention to discerning when "direct amends" is the answer or when some internal work needs to be done. She needed to "mend" that part of her that felt unlovable and that wanted to be held. She needed to grieve the loss of her relationship and learn that being alone does not make her unworthy of love. She did not need to burden Jake with another phone call in the hope that he would make her feel better. However, this experience now serves as a reminder to Frieda to play the amends all the way through before she approaches someone with this Step. Looking at all of the ways someone might respond to her helps her to see whether her motives are in alignment with the principle of the Ninth Step.

Magical Thinking

Magical thinking centers on one's belief system rather than on the facts. One example of magical thinking can be seen in studies that elicit the placebo effect. When someone is taking a sugar pill for what ails him and *believes* it has medicinal properties, sometimes he actually has symptom relief. Magical thinking as spiritual bypass occurs when someone uses his beliefs about a ritual or idea to override the facts of his emotional experience.

Lindsey realized she was experiencing magical thinking when she came to therapy. She had been in Al-Anon for more than five years and found that she was still preoccupied with fear and anxiety. To combat her worries, Lindsey mentioned that she had recently started sleeping with a crystal that she was told had healing properties for transforming negative energies into positive ones. She wanted to transform her negative memories of the past into positive affirmations for her future.

Lindsey particularly appreciated that this practice could happen while she was sleeping. Having glimpsed the emotional upset that occurred when she faced her past, engaging with her painful memories in this passive way felt much safer to her. Yet she knew she needed to do something to find more personal freedom in her life because, despite her intellectual understanding of everything that she had been through, the overwhelming feelings remained.

Lindsey ultimately realized the crystal was not going to erase her feelings any more than her intellect could. She needed to honor how she was feeling instead of finding ways to transcend it. From such a place of acceptance, she recalled that she often heard "just get over it" as a child, and she could see how she was now saying the same thing to herself. She expected herself to "get over it" by any means possible, including Al-Anon, the Steps and tools, and her spiritual practice of working with crystals. In this way, Lindsey was bypassing her present experience. She didn't have permission to be who she was, which kept her stuck in her fear and anxiety.

When Lindsey stopped seeing the crystal as something magical that would remove her history and her vulnerability, she saw how the same object could be used to help her engage with her worries. The precious stone could represent her intention for healing and her belief that healing was possible. The crystal went from being a talisman of distraction and procrastination to becoming a sacred touchstone Lindsey could use to dip her toes into that which had previously been too scary. Sleeping with the crystal wouldn't remedy her fears, but it could allow her to feel a sense of protection while she faced them. Her story highlights the difference between magical thinking about symbols and rituals and how one can use these in a meaningful and fruitful manner. Even though she still hopes her pain might disappear altogether, she is becoming incrementally closer to God and to herself in the process. She vacillates between the two poles of wanting the crystal to remove her obstacles and knowing it is a tool that can help her navigate through them.

Lindsey's crystal could be replaced with any sort of symbol, idea, ritual, or belief system. Her experience shows us once again that spiritual bypass only prolongs a person's suffering and that healthy spiritual practice involves working with the human condition, not overriding it.

The Steps and the Tools

As we have seen, people in recovery can use the Steps and the tools of the program as a way of controlling (or bypassing) their feelings. Doing something can make a person feel she is getting closer to the other side of an issue, which is often preferable to being in the middle where things are unclear, confusing, and uncomfortable. An example of using the Steps to control a situation can be seen in Ellen's story.

Ellen was a willing client in therapy, to the extent that she never thought she was working hard enough. She was rather hard on herself and asked that I point out any flaws I might witness on a regular basis. She was intelligent and analytical, and she could express how she was feeling quite beautifully, but the words often seemed like a shield for the actual feelings that lay below the surface.

Ellen had been in several Twelve Step programs for more than ten years when she came to therapy. She had also seen several other therapists during her life, so she was no stranger to the practice. She was coming to therapy at this time because she had recently moved in with her partner and that commitment was bringing up a lot of anxiety. In addition to coming to therapy, Ellen was working the Steps with her sponsor. During one of our sessions, she brought in some writing she had done for her Fourth Step: "Made a searching and fearless moral inventory of ourselves."

Ellen had clearly spent a lot of time writing out her inventory, and as she was quite familiar with the process, she was able to deeply investigate what she thought her contributions were to her experience of fears and resentments (her part). Although I was impressed with her writing, I found myself unable to believe what Ellen was saying. It was as though she made an intellectual guess at her part, but it didn't have any feeling attached to it. It didn't come from the heart. She was able to plug in the words that were suggested in the Big Book about what was being affected in her—her self-esteem, ambition, security, etc.—but the words didn't seem to truly resonate. It felt as though Ellen was digging for an answer that would get her through her current painful feelings because she desperately wanted to be on the other side.

I gently expressed these thoughts to Ellen, and she began to cry. I could see how sensitive she was to this topic and that, although she understood what I was saying, she had a lot of shame about it. She clearly did not intend to bypass her feelings. Ellen truly believed she was working a good program and she couldn't comprehend that she had somehow used the Fourth Step for its unintended purpose. Her sensitivity and shame is a reminder that spiritual bypass is a defense—not a conscious process—thereby making it a delicate subject when the individual first becomes aware of her underlying drives. As sponsors, friends, or therapists, we need to be very careful about how we engage with people who are seemingly in spiritual bypass, because they are likely to defend themselves even more if they feel they are being judged. Perhaps you can recall a time in your own life when someone pointed out something that you weren't quite ready to hear.

In discussing the inventory process, Ellen eventually came to see that her motives for doing the writing were about getting rid of the bad feelings that surrounded her fears and resentments. She thought she wouldn't have to feel them if she uncovered what she had done to create them in the first place. She hoped that if she made the inventory all about her part, where she had a sense of control, she could find some relief. Although she felt some initial relief in doing the writing, this was only temporary and all of her feelings eventually came back.

Ellen learned that she is not capable of escaping her feelings but that she can tolerate them. She remembered methods that had helped her to be present to herself and to her experience in the past, including sharing how she felt with others. She had a tendency to feel that, because she had long-term recovery, she shouldn't have to continually share about her feelings, especially if they seemed to be lasting a long time. She feared that she would be perceived as a broken record or that she would burn out people with her pain. She discovered that people are much more generous with their time and attention than she ever imagined possible. Additionally, she came to see that by sharing her pain, she gave others permission to do the same. Ellen also remembered that listening to music is a powerful way to feel and express her feelings. She could dance in her own living room or sing at the top of her lungs. She could watch a sad movie or engage in any creative outlet as a way of feeling her feelings. All of these are ways for her to be present to what she is feeling, without trying to change it or to jump to some imaginary finish line.

Isolation

"Almost without exception, alcoholics are tortured by loneliness. Even before our drinking got bad and people began to cut us off, nearly all of us suffered the feeling that we didn't quite belong."

—— BILL W.

Isolation is another way people attempt to maintain a sense of control in recovery. Prior to her relapse, Chelsea was holding on to control by making sure nobody in AA really knew who she was. Eventually, she came to personally understand the AA adage "You're as sick as your secrets," which means that building community and honest connections with others is an important factor in finding interpersonal peace and harmony.

In terms of spiritual bypass, isolation occurs when someone wants to project that he is "fine." If he can keep his world small, where no one can see it, it is easier to look spiritually and emotionally sound. No one can see the pain or fears. He can insert himself into conversation or share at meetings when he has a "solution" to add, but even in a crowd, he keeps his true self hidden. Unfortunately, this strategy is as useful as the diet tip that suggests if no one saw you eat it, the calories don't count.

We often isolate out of shame; we don't really want people to know that we feel like a fraud or that we are afraid. We don't want to feel judged, because we are already so hard on ourselves. Of course, when someone actually admits these things at a meeting, most of those in attendance start laughing or nodding their heads in agreement. Most people feel this way, and having it said out loud is such a relief! But the isolator still sneaks out the door without having truly unburdened himself.

Although isolation can indeed be a form of spiritual bypass, it is important to distinguish it from taking healthy alone time. As with most of the concepts we've considered, there are at least two sides to the story. Although Allison was isolating from the world in early sobriety, this was an attempt to protect herself from relapse. She knew that if she continued hanging out with the same people she used to, she would be prone to using again. Eventually, when she had established enough recovery, she was able to break her isolation and join society again. One way of navigating your own need for alone time is to ask yourself what your motives are. If you are exhausted, you have overextended yourself, or you feel out of touch with yourself, you are probably in need of some alone time. This is self-care, not spiritual bypass. If you feel afraid, anxious, or irritated, you might be isolating in a way that can lead to spiritual bypass.

In Conclusion

Many control-seeking strategies and behaviors are signals of spiritual bypass. Perhaps you recognized yourself in some of the examples given, or you might find yourself identifying with them one day. Most people find it easier to see and identify these things in other people than in themselves. Whatever your experience, let these stories and examples seep into your consciousness and trust that, should your process involve spiritual bypass, you will be given everything you need to take you where you are meant to go.

TWELVE

Becoming Right Size

"Having been granted a perfect release from alcoholism, why then shouldn't we be able to achieve by the same means a perfect release from every other difficulty or defect? This is the riddle of our existence."

— Bill W.

A S THE PARTICIPANTS in my study revealed what it was like, what happened, and what it is like now with regard to spiritual bypass, it became clear that two components were absolutely necessary to move through their reliance on that defense: humility and acceptance. Part one of this book highlighted the addict's tendency toward narcissism and grandiosity. These personality traits are one reason AA places great emphasis on gaining humility and acceptance to maintain sobriety, because these qualities can counteract the adverse effects of a person's temperament. These same qualities can also counteract the negative effects of developing unrealistic expectations of sobriety.

Humility

Before we discuss humility, let's review some definitions from *Twelve Steps and Twelve Traditions*:

> *Humility*—a word often misunderstood. To those who have made progress in A.A., it amounts to a clear recognition of what and who we really are, followed by a sincere attempt to become what we could be.

The attainment of greater humility is the foundation principle of each of A.A.'s Twelve Steps. For without some degree of humility, no alcoholic can stay sober at all. Nearly all A.A.'s have found, too, that unless they develop much more of this precious quality than may be required just for sobriety, they still haven't much chance of becoming truly happy. Without it, they cannot live to much useful purpose, or, in adversity, be able to summon the faith that can meet any emergency.

That basic ingredient of all humility, a desire to seek and do God's will . . .

To get completely away from our aversion to the idea of being humble, to gain a vision of humility as the avenue to true freedom of the human spirit, to be willing to work for humility as something to be desired for itself, takes most of us a long, long time. A whole lifetime geared to self-centeredness cannot be set in reverse all at once.

An important key to maintaining sobriety and to overcoming spiritual bypass is acquiring humility. Recognizing oneself as no better, or no less, than anyone else can penetrate the bubble of an inflated sense of self. Humility can enable a recovering person to be honest, to ask for help, to rely on a Higher Power, to accept his fallibility, and to appreciate the full spectrum of human experience. I particularly appreciate how the above passages not only reference humility as vital for recovery, but as a lifelong endeavor.

Initially, Allison recognized that a lack of humility led to her experiences of spiritual bypass. She saw that, conversely, gaining humility was one way of breaking through the defense. She sought humility by attempting to release the illusion that she could control her Higher Power and by simultaneously recognizing her feelings of powerlessness about money and material success. The combination of these two experiences led to her becoming a newcomer in Debtors Anonymous (DA), which provided an opportunity to accept her current circumstances, to create a new conception of her Higher Power, and to strengthen her relationship to that Higher Power. Allison continues to strive for humility by enlarging her connection with God in times of stress as well as prosperity, by listening for direction in her prayer and meditation, and by continuing to "pause" before she takes impulsive actions.

Bradford's story showed us that finding humility was the key to moving through his spiritual bypass, because when he saw himself for who he really was, and not who he thought he should be, he found unconditional love for himself and his fellows. He became "right size." He no longer needed to bypass his feelings because he was acknowledging the fullness of himself, including the little boy who remained inside.

Being humble means owning your gifts and your frailties and turning them all over to your Higher Power. Every inventory, every phone call to your sponsor, every act of service, every moment in every day contains an opportunity to be humble. It is such a gift to know that we can continually practice gaining this essential quality and that the minute we think we've "got it," we know that we need to keep working on it.

Acceptance

"The spiritual journey is not about heaven and finally getting to a place that's really swell."

— PEMA CHÖDRÖN, WHEN THINGS FALL APART

Because spiritual bypass is an attempt to avoid one's painful feelings, a way to break through the defense is by accepting everything that you are experiencing and feeling. This point cannot be highlighted enough. If a recovering alcoholic believes that sobriety, or spiritual practice, should produce "happy, joyous, and free" feelings all the time, she will need to redefine recovery to include the darker aspects of emotional experience. It is by honoring her feelings that a personal experience of "this too shall pass" becomes possible. It is also through experiencing one's feelings that growth, development, and self-acceptance can occur. Tools that promote acceptance of one's feelings are attendance at meetings where others are sharing the truth of their experience rather than only the positive highlights, sharing one's own struggles as they are happening, becoming vulnerable with others, and praying for the willingness to see and know the truth about oneself no matter what it looks like.

If you have been in the program for any length of time, you have probably heard the reference to "acceptance" in *Alcoholics Anonymous* (see page 449 of the third edition or page 417 of the fourth edition):

> And acceptance is the answer to *all* my problems today. When I am disturbed, it is because I find some person, place, thing, or situation—some fact of my life—unacceptable to me, and I can find no serenity until I accept that person, place, thing, or situation as being exactly the way it is supposed to be at this moment. Nothing, absolutely nothing, happens in God's world by mistake. Until I could accept my alcoholism, I could not stay sober; unless I accept life completely on life's terms, I cannot be happy.

If you have obtained some sobriety, you can undoubtedly relate to this passage—accepting that you are powerless becomes the threshold to a new, positive experience in recovery. Acceptance can indeed relieve one's suffering.

However, I want to challenge the idea that acceptance will always bring happiness or that acceptance means aligning yourself with a positive viewpoint on a particular subject. This interpretation is often held when people read that Big Book passage. Although acceptance can sometimes bring happiness, believing that it should *always* make one happy is a potential for spiritual bypass.

Acceptance simply means to acknowledge the entire truth about something. It is not related to how you feel about it all. It might mean that, rather than feeling good about a situation, you learn to tolerate it. You might eventually develop a positive perspective, but it will be a result of accepting things exactly as they are. We can still strive to be good human beings, to treat people with kindness, and to do the "next right thing," but we are entitled to feel all of our feelings along the way. The reason acceptance often brings some relief is that the person no longer struggles against what is real. He may not love his circumstances, but at least he isn't adding insult to injury by ignoring, pretending, or fighting with them.

I know a woman who absolutely accepted that she was an alcoholic and went to at least one meeting, if not two, every day for the entire first year of her sobriety. All the acceptance and willingness she could muster did not bring her happiness. She was struggling with painful memories from her past, she was coping with the effects of pervasive trauma, and she wanted to drink every single day. She accepted that these were her issues to face when she got sober, but it did not immediately render her contented or joyful.

An example of acceptance being misinterpreted is when people proclaim that "acceptance is the answer to *all* my problems" means a person should have no ill feelings about physical, sexual, or emotional abuse he survived. In this way, he may conflate acceptance with healing—healing that may take a lifetime to achieve. Although acceptance is a useful idea, like all the other tools mentioned in this book, it is not a universal remedy. Accepting the death of a loved one or the loss of a job or a diagnosis of cancer does not take away the grieving process. However, acceptance can enable someone to show up for the grieving process. Accepting that you have myriad feelings can give you permission to feel them. Accepting that life is in session can enable you to share the journey with those around you.

We saw examples of the power in accepting all of one's feelings and experiences in the personal stories outlined in part one of this book. Additionally, Jack Kornfield encourages us to face the totality of our experiences to find real healing. Ram Dass's story exemplified the need to fully accept humanity to be in true harmony with the way of things. All of these point to the same conclusion: humility and acceptance are the keys to moving through spiritual bypass.

The Balancing Act

"To be doomed to an alcoholic death or to live on a spiritual basis are not always easy alternatives to face."

—— BILL W.

At some point in recovery, for some people abstinence from alcohol can begin to be taken for granted, and *sobriety* begins to be defined through a perceived entitlement to a better life, above and beyond not drinking. Individuals lose sight of the time when they only desired the ability to stay sober and may forget their past powerlessness to make it happen. Gifted with sobriety, the recovering person nevertheless retains his self-centered nature, and the prospect of living "life on life's terms" may seem intolerable. We saw an example of this in Chelsea's story when she had the expectation that she would be relieved of all unwanted situations and that she was entitled to a life that continually looked and felt better. Chelsea once admitted at an AA meeting, "If somebody had told me that at ten years sober, this is what it would look like, I wouldn't have quit drinking." In fact, it may have been Chelsea's willingness to admit her unhappiness that allowed her to realign her expectations.

Each participant involved in my study developed unrealistic expectations about what sobriety should afford him or her. One explanation for this tendency can be found in Abraham Maslow's hierarchy of needs. Maslow is considered the father of humanistic psychology and he created a model that depicts our motivation and orientation to needs and wants. In speaking about the hierarchy of needs, Maslow (as cited by Koltko-Rivera) stated,

It is quite true that man lives by bread alone—when there is no bread. But what happens to man's desires when there is plenty of bread and when his belly is chronically filled?

> At once other (and "higher") needs emerge and these, rather than physiological hungers, dominate the organism. And when these in turn are satisfied, again new (and still "higher") needs emerge and so on.

This description helps us understand how an alcoholic might continue to strive toward fulfilling greater needs and desires as he remains sober. Each recovering person was, at one time, unable to stop drinking. The most one could hope for at such an early stage would be to stay clean one day at a time. Envisioning anything beyond fulfilling this basic need can seem impossible in early sobriety. However, once the addict has a strong foundation of abstinence, new and "higher" needs emerge. For people in recovery, this progression needs to be tempered. It requires a delicate balance of striving for the fulfillment of greater needs while maintaining reverence for their current sobriety.

One example of spiritual bypass and unrealistic expectations in recovery can be seen in the story of my client Keith. Keith was struggling with his primary relationships and could see how his selfishness was getting in the way of a lasting partnership with his girlfriend. To become clearer about how and why this continued to happen, Keith vigorously worked Steps Six and Seven: "Were entirely ready to have God remove all these defects of character" and "Humbly asked Him to remove our shortcomings." He had a belief that if he were truly ready to look at his defects and to have them removed, he would be blessed with unselfish behavior and his girlfriend would stay with him.

Keith read every word in Steps Six and Seven, and he worked diligently with his sponsor. He took full responsibility for his character defects and he recited the Seventh Step prayer several times a day:

My Creator, I am now willing that you should have all of me, good and bad. I pray that you now remove from me every single defect of character which stands in the way of my usefulness to you and my fellows. Grant me strength, as I go out from here, to do your bidding. Amen.

Keith desperately wanted his defects removed and he was doing everything in his power to change his ways. However, in the end, his girlfriend still decided to leave. He was devastated and furious. He felt he had done all that was asked of him, and still his relationship ended.

What Keith couldn't see until many years later was that his character defect of selfishness was running the show in getting rid of his character defects! He wanted what he wanted, when he wanted it. He spent more time focusing on himself and getting his needs met than in leaning into his relationship and spending time with his girlfriend. He was "doing the work" to gain a particular outcome instead of being present with his circumstances and the corresponding feelings. In hindsight, Keith could see that he viewed his program as a magic bullet for everything in his life. He had an expectation that if he showed up and applied the Steps, things would go according to his plan. This was a humbling lesson for Keith, one that allowed him to find some real balance in his life. Rather than using the Seventh Step prayer as a means of getting what he wanted, he went back to reciting the Serenity Prayer to help him maintain some equanimity:

God grant me the serenity
to accept the things I cannot change,
courage to change the things I can,
and the wisdom to know the difference.

Finding and maintaining balance is a tall order for people in recovery—and, let's face it, for all people in general. I have worked with many addicts who struggle with how many meetings to attend and other questions related to what is checking *in* and what is checking *out*. Does someone need to be sitting in more meetings so she can show up for the rest of life, or is attending more meetings a way of ignoring what is waiting for her at home? There is also the balance between Twelve Step work and using outside help such as religious services, therapy, and physical practices like yoga or going to the gym. And of course, we can't forget about spending time in nature, having fun, and just relaxing. So many addicts don't know how to have fun when they get sober, and they feel like they need to be "good girls and boys" to make up for lost time.

Although no quick and easy solution exists for finding your perfect balance between gratitude for recovery and striving for more—or for balancing recovery with the rest of your life—I have always enjoyed the AA reference to Rule 62: "Don't take yourself too damn seriously."

THIRTEEN

Integration Leads to Integrity

"Finally I am coming to the conclusion that my highest ambition is to be what I already am. That I will never fulfill my obligation to surpass myself unless I first accept myself, and if I accept myself fully in the right way, I will already have surpassed myself."

— THOMAS MERTON

I
N ESSENCE, INTEGRATION IS THE FRUIT of humility and acceptance. It is based on the root word *integrity*, which is defined as wholeness, soundness, and one's possession of high moral standards. In the context of this book, integrating both the light and dark aspects of one's self is an essential component to experiencing a psychic change—psychological and spiritual recovery—in the program. Integrating the fullness of the human condition into one's spiritual practice is what leads to emotional sobriety.

Optimal recovery hinges on the AA adage "Faith without works is dead" and the recognition that healing must occur physically, emotionally, and spiritually. Abstaining from alcohol one day at a time can be seen as the foundation on which spiritual and psychological recovery can be built. For some, a spiritual awakening is required for the emotional work to become possible. For others, investigating psychological roadblocks gives way to spiritual pursuits. To experience a psychic change, and to work through spiritual bypass, a recovering alcoholic must take action on all three fronts. In this way, second-stage recovery is a perpetually integrative process.

The results from my research confirmed repeatedly that recovery is about embracing the truth of who we are. It begins with a person recognizing that he is an alcoholic. Owning his disease of addiction needs to occur before further recovery can commence. In this process, the alcoholic can come to know the difference between being an active addict or a sober one. This points to the intrinsic benefit of integration, in that it enables consciousness, which enables choice. Choosing recovery means that a person can be an alcoholic and also be sober in mind, body, and spirit.

Compartmentalizing is the opposite of integration. If a person is compartmentalizing, she might think that admitting she has the disease of alcoholism would define her as a whole. Compartmentalizing is like putting the blinders on, in that you can't see the truth and choices around you but only what you perceive to be right in front of you. This type of thinking keeps a person's experiences relatively limited because there is an inability to see the big picture. I have always loved the following quote as a reminder of the inherent value of the big picture: "The brightest stars are in the darkest sky." We can only see the stars if we widen our vision and perception from the small points of darkness that we are usually drawn toward. We can additionally interpret this quote to mean that in owning one's darkness a person can finally see the fiery gems that have been there all along. Imperfections are intrinsically valuable and can be one's greatest teacher by fueling growth and development. Compartmentalizing keeps a person focused on the problem; integration opens a person to vast possibilities.

I have often shared with clients who are afraid of seeing and experiencing the big picture that our emotions are on one large continuum. When we access one part of the spectrum, we simultaneously open the possibility to express and feel emotion on the other end. To know and digest our hurt allows us to know and express our joy. The darkness eventually leads to the light. A mentor of mine would often remind me, as I had the feeling that I was walking into darkness (as though I were in a deep and scary cave), that there is gold in the depths of that journey. She was right every single time.

I appreciate the idea that this *is* the gift of free will. We are given the ability to experience it all. I know the feeling of joy only because I have the ability to compare and contrast it with the feeling of pain. If these are the gifts of free will, I would extend this same philosophy to recovery—in which the ability to feel hurt, loneliness, and sadness are actually gifts. They are essential building blocks of life that connect us to the rest of ourself and to one another. This is why people can recover by sharing their experience, strength, and hope with one another—because other people identify, they understand, they relate, and they grow. I do not relate to the person who never feels let down or sorrowful or jealous. Maybe it's just me, but I feel those things. And those same feelings can be sitting right beside feelings of gratitude, compassion, and curiosity. None of these feelings are mutually exclusive.

Thus far we have been talking about integrating our feelings to access a larger and freer experience of the world. Now let's take this same idea and apply it to the integration of the physical self, the mind, and the spirit. In *Toward a Psychology of Awakening,* John Welwood wrote that throughout his career he has witnessed people who were spiritual warriors on one hand, while emotionally immature on the other:

> I have often been struck by the huge gap between the sophistication of their spiritual practice and the level of their personal development. Some of them have spent years doing what were once considered the most advanced, esoteric practices, reserved only for the select few in traditional Asia, without developing the most rudimentary forms of self-love or interpersonal sensitivity.

People in recovery often witness others with long-term sobriety who are psychologically defended or who have poor health due to poor eating habits, lack of exercise, or cigarette smoking. Although the AA tenet of "Progress, not perfection" certainly leaves room for people to be who and what they are, second-stage recovery is about applying the principles in a holistic fashion. The intention is to widen the comfort zone and to expand in health and wholeness not just spiritually, but emotionally and physically as well. As sobriety ceases to be defined through abstinence alone, you can see why recovery is a lifetime journey. There is always room to grow—always room to integrate another facet of one's self and to "practice these principles in all our affairs."

Putting It All Together

KNOW ENOUGH TO KNOW that I cannot answer the big questions in this life. But I can speak to what we have already come to discover. Being a human being is a wondrous experience. We are individuals with families, friends, neighbors, co-workers, and enemies. We have bodies that are tall and short, healthy and sick. We have feelings and thoughts, goals and dreams, heartaches and misery. Each of us is like a snowflake or a piece of one giant puzzle. We see things from our own particular vantage points, from our own personal experiences, with our own intellects, values, and cultures. Amid all the mystery and peculiarity, we create a life for ourselves—and we build a story about the life we have created and how it fits into the big picture of things. In an attempt to feel a little more secure and a little less vulnerable, we try to find a simple path on which to walk. We wish that all of the complicated mess of life could be contained, so we create strategies to do so. We wish for all the wrinkles to be ironed out and all the struggles to be overcome.

If you are sober, abstinent, clean, debt-free, smoke-free, or generally keeping your side of the street clean by working a Twelve Step program, congratulations. These are amazing accomplishments given everything that you're up against. Sobriety on any level is worthy of celebration if you have ever been powerless over substances or behaviors that have led to addiction. Seriously, if you have found a way to arrest your debilitating addiction, take a moment to honor all that means for you.

I hope that this book can bring a celebration of sobriety back to the forefront. You are clean today and that is extraordinary. Regardless of what else is going on, whether you are happy or sad, feeling lost or found, if you aren't using, I say "Bravo!" It seems to me that somewhere along the road of recovery, a split has occurred between active addiction as tied to all things unpleasant and recovery being equated with all things grand. Such a split is artificial. We know that this is just black-and-white thinking. Chasing recovery as a means of not ever feeling uncomfortable or afraid or confused is unrealistic to say the least. But part of us has wanted to believe it anyway. From *Twelve Steps and Twelve Traditions*:

> It is nowhere evident, at least in this life, that our Creator expects us fully to eliminate our instinctual drives. So far as we know, it is nowhere on the record that God has completely removed from any human being all his natural drives.

I hope that learning about spiritual bypass has expanded your knowledge of second-stage recovery and given you permission to be human. That this information allows you to be more current in your thinking about the program and your relationship to it. That you have a greater understanding of the subtle ways in which recovery can be mistaken for a means to perfect spiritual, psychological, physical, financial health and well-being. I hope your familiarity with the themes related to spiritual bypass will provide new guidelines for your own recovery. That you will be better able to accept that we will always have unconscious drives and fears, even as we gain greater access to our true self and our highest capacities. One way of honoring this distinction is to see spiritual bypass as both adaptive and maladaptive.

Adaptive experiences of spiritual bypass can provide you with a sense of protection from relapse and a safeguard from emotions that might be too overwhelming to feel at a particular time. If we were faced with Truth (with a capital T) or realizing all of our dreams in one sitting, we would probably become psychotic. Defenses are defending us from that potential. The slower portion of the adage "Sometimes quickly, sometimes slowly" tends to be the more sustainable of the two. So using spiritual practices or ideas defensively can be a useful experience in recovery: a person can maintain physical sobriety long enough for deeper issues to be addressed at a later time. This adaptive experience of spiritual bypass can be reexperienced throughout one's recovery as more layers of protection and resistance are removed—primarily through gaining humility and acceptance. From the perspective that all defense mechanisms can be helpful to some degree, spiritual bypass can positively contribute to a person's recovery in Twelve Step programs.

A defense mechanism becomes maladaptive when it has overstayed its usefulness, when it becomes rigid and is getting in the way of a person's development. One way of identifying spiritual bypass in this context is to see whether the Serenity Prayer has been inverted. For example, here is the original Serenity Prayer:

> God grant me the serenity
> to accept the things I cannot change,
> courage to change the things I can,
> and the wisdom to know the difference.
> Thy will, not mine, be done.

Someone experiencing spiritual bypass might unconsciously believe the Serenity Prayer expresses this instead:

> God grant me the courage
> to change the things I cannot accept,
> and the ability to achieve serenity
> no matter what I'm feeling.
> My will—with your help—be done.

Michael Beckwith speaks to the inherent difficulty in mal-adaptive spiritual bypass in the following quote from *Spiritual Liberation*:

> When you seek a spiritual path because it will "fix" you, it then becomes just another gimmick, a medicine to cure what ails you. . . . You will live in polarity, constantly pitting the "good" self against the "bad" self. . . . An authentic spiritual path will always give you back to yourself by providing the tools for self-realization, for self-empowerment.

I want to remind you that when it comes to emotional sobriety and your perpetual defenses, the rule is still "Progress, not perfection." Throughout the process of writing this book, I have continually confronted ways in which I am still defended on my spiritual path, and I am considered an "expert" on this topic. But that is precisely the point—by looking at all of the complexities of spiritual bypass, I have been able to free myself from some of the places where I have been stuck. I have come to integrate more of my shadow and to appreciate the chaos and craziness that is my life. I know that life includes "happy, joyous, and free" experiences—but that these are not static states. I am not defined by these experiences, just as I am not defined by being an "expert." I have been reminded that "success" is about living courageously in the process, throughout the ups and downs. And I know that there is much more that I will uncover in the future. I hope that your investigation of spiritual bypass will yield similar results.

Believing that God will reward good behavior if you take the right action and turn over the results is really just superstitious thinking. God isn't only in the results. He is in the action too. God—whether you refer to Universe, Goddess, Love, Fullness, Emptiness, Divine Order, or another term—was there all day yesterday, whether we sought out the connection or not, whether we feel good about our behavior or not. And God is in this moment, and this moment, and this one. I have always liked the saying "God can move mountains but we have to carry the shovel," but it has often left me wondering: what size shovel should I have and how fast should I be shoveling? I guess that God is in the shovel, too, and in each breath and each step that I take. There really is no separation between me—that is, my actions and my emotions—and God. Even in addiction, even in "mistakes," even in misfortune, God is in those too. Not just moving mountains to help us to overcome but in our ability to surrender to whatever is happening, no matter what it looks like, God is in there.

One of the greatest spiritual teachings in AA is to take things "one day at a time." This philosophy allows us to handle anything if it is broken down into a manageable time frame. An alcoholic might not be able to stay sober for the rest of his life, but he can stay sober for this day, or this hour, or this minute. The program teaches people to be present to their life and to live in the moment. That is all we have anyway. A friend of mine once said, "Ingrid, you can't grieve in advance." It took me a while to appreciate the wisdom in that sentence. She meant that even in the possibility of someone's death, I cannot really grieve until that person has passed on. I can't feel my feelings in advance. I can't prepare enough, know enough, be enough, rise above enough to shield myself from the things that are painful. But I can do my best to be present for what is happening right in front of me. Even if that thing is tragedy and even if I can only do it for one minute at a time.

May you, and the many Twelve Step programs as a whole, continue to blossom into the fullest expressions of what the founders envisioned. From Step Twelve in *Twelve Steps and Twelve Traditions*, consider:

> Can we now accept poverty, sickness, loneliness, and bereavement with courage and serenity? Can we steadfastly content ourselves with the humbler, yet sometimes more durable, satisfactions when the brighter, more glittering achievements are denied us?

> The A.A. answer to these questions about living is "Yes, all of these things are possible."

I end this book knowing that it is really just another beginning. It is beginning the conversation about spiritual bypass at the group level. I look forward to hearing how this material continues to grow and change as the collective group conscience has a voice in the matter. I know that my own experience and understanding of spiritual development will continue to evolve long after this book is printed and that these are the real "cash and prizes" in my life.

I would like to close this book with a poem by Mary Oliver and with gratitude for all of the gifts I have been given by leaning into my own humanity, to my imperfections, to my spiritual nature, and to my fellow travelers who inspire me to lean in a little more.

Wild Geese
by Mary Oliver

You do not have to be good.
You do not have to walk on your knees
for a hundred miles through the desert repenting.
You only have to let the soft animal of your body
    love what it loves.
Tell me about despair, yours, and I will tell you mine.
Meanwhile the world goes on.
Meanwhile the sun and the clear pebbles of the rain
are moving across the landscapes,
over the prairies and the deep trees,
the mountains and the rivers.
Meanwhile the wild geese, high in the clean blue air,
are heading home again.
Whoever you are, no matter how lonely,
the world offers itself to your imagination,
calls to you like the wild geese, harsh and exciting—
over and over announcing your place
in the family of things.

The Hoop
Is Wider
Than You Think

"Badness is only spoiled goodness."

— C. S. LEWIS

THE PERSISTENT EVIDENCE IN MY RESEARCH that spiritual bypass can act as a healthy transitional period in someone's recovery was astonishing to discover. This idea was nowhere on my radar screen prior to conducting this study. My original literature review on spiritual bypass did not include anything related to psychospiritual development. I was partially influenced in that omission by countless graduate courses that included a discussion on spiritual bypass only as a pitfall. In my view, the take-home message for transpersonal psychologists was that spiritual bypass was hazardous to your health. From this perspective, I truly wanted to find a way for addicts in recovery to avoid the dangerous trap that seemed embedded in their spiritual journey. Fortunately, I chose a research method that forced me to suspend my preconceived ideas. I had to table what I thought I already knew if I were to discover what was actually going on with regard to spiritual bypass.

It was only after sitting with this material for quite some time that I began to evaluate my own relationship to spiritual bypass in a deeper way. I discovered that, although slightly embarrassing, my experiences of the defense had not obscured my spiritual path, nor had they limited my emotional growth and development. Spiritual bypass was one aspect of an entire picture. It was upon this discovery that my mission to help people avoid spiritual bypass became forever altered. I still wanted to spread the word about the defense mechanism and to alert people to its inherent challenges, but I now wanted to expand the definition of spiritual bypass altogether.

The irony of it is that my personal experience of initially constructing and conducting this research, assuming that it would yield certain results, was a bypass in and of itself. I wanted to carry out my research without being fully present to unseen possibilities. I didn't want to be vulnerable to the unknown. I wanted to confirm my hypothesis! Assuming that I already knew the answers and conducting research to confirm them was like thinking that I know what is best and praying for it to happen. Neither involves any acceptance of what is actually going on. There is no room for mystery or real inquiry, only a false sense of control because I'm "in the know."

In many ways, my personal experience mirrored that of the participants in my research. Just as they had to ask themselves what certain spiritual principles meant in order to fully comprehend and integrate them, I had to do the same with spiritual bypass. It was through this necessary process of first identifying with the culture's norms—thinking that bypass was strictly a pitfall—and then examining the personal dissonance that resulted that led me to a new level of understanding. In other words, I took what I initially understood as fact and then had to go beyond this comfortable resting place. I had to ask myself what I really thought and felt, despite evidence to the contrary. I had to remain open.

Understanding spiritual bypass as more than a pitfall has yielded results far beyond my initial aspiration. To consider that there is no point of arrival in recovery, that growth and development are occurring even when one feels "stuck," and that the darker aspects of human experience hold great value all provide permission to recovering alcoholics to be human beings among other human beings. This permission can be lifesaving for individuals who often feel enormous pressure to overcome their past, to make up for lost time, and to align with spiritual ideology in the hope that it will render them worthy of life's joys. What a gift to know continual growth is not an entirely conscious process that needs to be relentlessly managed and to understand there will be defenses at work, there will be countless experiences of discomfort, and the presence of these conditions does not necessarily signal pathology. Instead it can be considered a constellation of markers indicating a cyclical stage of healthy development!

As with any defense mechanism, spiritual bypass can aid a person in defending against anxiety or other stressors. For a recovering alcoholic, the ability to avoid certain stressors may provide an opportunity to obtain abstinence. This abstinence can then become a foundation from which it is possible to access more of her emotional experience. Spiritual bypass employed in this manner serves as a container for, or transition to, greater development. It is a stepping-stone rather than a stumbling block.

The once-terrifying notion of spiritual bypass as spiritual suicide has been redefined with every draft of this book I have written and every experience that I have allowed myself to linger with a little bit longer. I am noticing just how wide the hoop is in my own spiritual journey and am grateful for this ever-evolving understanding. I don't have to be "good" or "right" to be spiritual. I don't need to achieve certain results to confirm that I'm on the appropriate path. I don't have to legitimize my spirituality through achievements or successes. Michael Beckwith speaks to this idea in *Spiritual Liberation*:

> When you move through life in a consciousness of "I'm all right already," you realize that you aren't moving from a state of imperfection to perfection, from incompletion to completion. Instead, you understand that you are moving from one point of development to the next.

I would like to extend this to people in recovery—that moving from active addiction to sobriety is not the same as moving from being bad to being good, but simply from one point of development to the next. And the same goes for early recovery, long-term recovery, and those considered "old-timers." Whatever stage you're at is simply another stage of development. Perhaps you can see that, even as you are experiencing being an old-timer, the experience itself is new and thus you are a *newcomer* as an old-timer.

Step Two of *Twelve Steps and Twelve Traditions* refers to the hoop one has to jump through to find a Higher Power. The AA founders wanted you to know that the hoop is much wider than you might think. People who have never had faith, or who had it and lost it, can find a path to sanity just as assuredly as people who have a strong sense of faith. *Twelve Steps and Twelve Traditions* doesn't suggest that you need to walk a tightrope to find recovery. It says that even atheists and agnostics have found they are able to work the Twelve Steps, finding sobriety and serenity. The program doesn't advise you to come into AA with a defined set of spiritual principles that work in your life. It says you can "come to believe."

The same is true regarding spiritual bypass. We can start from wherever we are and grow from there. I didn't have to know my research results before I ever conducted my first interview. I was allowed to be exactly who I was, with all of my preconceived ideas and with my desire to bypass all the unknowns. At the end of the day, I just had to be willing. Step Three in *Twelve Steps and Twelve Traditions* reads,

> Practicing Step Three is like the opening of a door which to all appearances is still closed and locked. All we need is a key, and the decision to swing the door open. There is only one key, and it is called willingness. Once unlocked by willingness, the door opens almost of itself, and looking through it, we shall see a pathway beside which is an inscription. It reads: "This is the way to a faith that works."

I am coming to believe that the hoop is much wider than we think in every area of life: for finding and redefining a spiritual path, for moving in and out of spiritual bypass, and for moving in and out of all the challenges that life brings. We need to make mistakes to learn that we can do things differently. I thank God that I couldn't pray my way to getting the research results I wanted: I would have never had the opportunity to discover so much about myself and the nature of the human condition and to share such rich, dynamic findings with people in recovery.

Bibliography

Adyashanti. *The End of Your World: Uncensored Straight Talk on the Nature of Enlightenment.* Boulder, CO: Sounds True, 2008.

Alcoholics Anonymous. *Alcoholics Anonymous Comes of Age.* New York: Alcoholics Anonymous World Services, 1957, pages 63–64.

_____. *Alcoholics Anonymous: The Story of How Many Thousands of Men and Women Have Recovered from Alcoholism* (4th ed.). New York: Alcoholics Anonymous World Services, 2001, pages 12, 44, 52, 62, 73, 76, 83–84, 130.

_____. *'Pass It On': The Story of Bill Wilson and How the A.A. Message Reached the World.* New York: Alcoholics Anonymous World Services, 1984, page 370.

_____. *Twelve Steps and Twelve Traditions.* New York: Alcoholics Anonymous World Services, 1995, pages 12, 34, 57–58, 64–65, 69–70, 72–73, 112.

Alcoholics Anonymous World Services Inc. *Questions & Answers on Sponsorship,* 2007. Retrieved February 20, 2007, from alcoholics-anonymous.org/en_information_aa.cfm?PageID=162; as of publication date, available at www.aa.org/lang/en/catalog .cfm?category=4&product=17) 1976, 1983, revised 2004, 2005.

B., Dick. "Alcoholics Anonymous History: Measuring AA Relapses & Successes." Retrieved May 9, 2010. http://dickb.com/relapses successes.shtml.

Battista, John R. "Offensive Spirituality and Spiritual Defenses." In *Textbook of Transpersonal Psychiatry and Psychology*, edited by Bruce W. Scotton, Allen B. Chinen, and John R. Battista, 250–260. New York: Basic Books, 1996.

Beckwith, Michael B. *Spiritual Liberation: Fulfilling Your Soul's Potential*. New York: Atria Books, 2008.

Carter, Toni M. "The Effects of Spiritual Practices on Recovery from Substance Abuse." *Journal of Psychiatric and Mental Health Nursing* 5, no. 5 (1998): 409–13.

Cashwell, Craig, Jane Myers, and W. Matthew Shurts. "Using the Developmental Counseling and Therapy Model to Work with a Client in Spiritual Bypass: Some Preliminary Considerations." *Journal of Counseling and Development*, no. 82 (2004): 403–9.

Cheever, Susan. *My Name Is Bill: Bill Wilson—His Life and the Creation of Alcoholics Anonymous*. New York: Washington Square Press, 2004.

Chödrön, Pema. *When Things Fall Apart: Heart Advice for Difficult Times*. Boston: Shambhala, 2000.

Cortright, Brant. *Psychotherapy and Spirit: Theory and Practice in Transpersonal Psychotherapy*. Albany: State University of New York Press, 1997.

Csanyi, Daniel A. "Faith Development and the Age of Readiness for the Bible." *Religious Education* 77, no. 5 (1982): 518–24.

Dass, Ram. "A Ten-Year Perspective." In *Spiritual Choices: The Problems of Recognizing Authentic Paths to Inner Transformation*, edited by Dick Anthony, Bruce Ecker, and Ken Wilber, 139–52. New York: Paragon House, 1987.

Ferrucci, Piero. *What We May Be: Techniques for Psychological and Spiritual Growth Through Psychosynthesis*. Los Angeles: J. P. Tarcher, 1982.

Finlay, Steven W. "Influence of Carl Jung and William James on the Origin of Alcoholics Anonymous." *Review of General Psychology* 4, no. 1 (2000): 3–12.

Firman, John, and Ann Gila. *Psychosynthesis: A Psychology of the Spirit*. Albany: State University of New York Press, 2002.

Fowler, James W. *Stages of Faith: The Psychology of Human Development and the Quest for Meaning.* San Francisco: HarperSanFrancisco, 1995.

Fox, Matthew. *Creation Spirituality: Liberating Gifts for the Peoples of the Earth.* San Francisco: HarperSanFrancisco, 1991.

Hart, Kenneth, and Cherry Huggett. "Narcissism: A Barrier to Personal Acceptance of the Spiritual Aspect of Alcoholics Anonymous." *Alcoholism Treatment Quarterly* 23, no. 4 (2005): 85–100.

Hartigan, Francis. *Bill W.: A Biography of Alcoholics Anonymous Cofounder Bill Wilson.* New York: Thomas Dunne Books, 2000.

Heise, Robin G., and Jean A. Steitz, "Religious Perfectionism versus Spiritual Growth." *Counseling and Values* 36, no. 1 (1991): 11–18.

Jung, Carl G. "A Psychological Approach to the Dogma of the Trinity." In *The Collected Works of C. G. Jung* (Vol. 11, 2nd ed.), edited by H. Read, M. Fordham, and G. Adler, 148–200. Princeton, NJ: Princeton University Press, 1969.

Koltko-Rivera, Mark E. "Rediscovering the Later Version of Maslow's Hierarchy of Needs: Self-Transcendence and Opportunities for Theory, Research, and Unification." *Review of General Psychology* 10, no. 4 (2006): 302–17.

Kornfield, Jack. "Even the Best Meditators Have Old Wounds to Heal: Combining Meditation and Psychotherapy." In *Paths Beyond Ego: The Transpersonal Vision,* edited by Roger Walsh and Frances Vaughan, 67–69. New York: Jeremy P. Tarcher/Putnam, 1993.

Kurtz, Ernest. *Not-God: A History of Alcoholics Anonymous.* Center City, MN: Hazelden Educational Services, 1979.

Kurtz, Ernest, and Katherine Ketcham. *The Spirituality of Imperfection: Storytelling and the Search for Meaning.* New York: Bantam Books, 1992.

Larsen, Earnie. *Stage II Recovery: Life Beyond Addiction.* San Francisco: HarperSanFrancisco, 1985.

Lewis, C. S. *The Case for Christianity.* Published in England as *Broadcast Talks.* New York: Macmillan, 1978.

Merton, Thomas. *New Seeds of Contemplation.* New York: New Directions, 1972.

Murray, Thomas S., Vanessa L. Malcarne, and Kathy Goggin. "Alcohol-Related God/Higher Power Control Beliefs, Locus of Control, and Recovery within the Alcoholics Anonymous Paradigm." *Alcoholism Treatment Quarterly* 21, no. 3 (2003): 23–39.

Nixon, Gary. "Beyond 'Dry Drunkenness': Facilitating Second Stage Recovery Using Wilber's 'Spectrum of Consciousness' Developmental Model." *Journal of Social Work Practice in the Addictions* 5, no. 3 (2005): 55–71.

Oliver. Mary. *Dream Work.* New York: Atlantic Monthly Press, 1986.

Peck, M. Scott. *The Different Drum.* New York: Touchstone/Simon and Schuster, 1987.

Ratliff, John. "Community Identity in an Alcoholics Anonymous Group: Discourse Contention and Integration." *Alcoholism Treatment Quarterly* 21, no. 3 (2003): 41–57.

Room, Robin, and Thomas Greenfield. "Alcoholics Anonymous, Other 12-Step Movements and Psychotherapy in the US Population, 1990." *Addiction* 88, no. 4 (1993): 555–62.

Sparks, Tav. "Transpersonal Treatment of Addictions: Radical Return to Roots." *ReVision: The Journal of Consciousness and Change* 10, no. 2 (1987): 49–64.

Taylor, Cheryl Zerbe. "Religious Addiction: Obsession with Spirituality." *Pastoral Psychology* 50, no. 4 (2002): 291–315.

Tiebout, Harry M. "The Act of Surrender in the Therapeutic Process." *Quarterly Journal of Studies on Alcohol,* 1949: 58–68 (retrieved from www.silkworth.net/tiebout/tiebout_surrender.html).

Trungpa, Chögyam. *Cutting Through Spiritual Materialism.* Boston: Shambhala, 2002.

Warfield, Robert D., and Marc B. Goldstein. "Spirituality: The Key to Recovery from Alcoholism." *Counseling and Values* 40, no. 3 (1996): 196–205.

Welwood, John. "Principles of Inner Work: Psychological and Spiritual." *The Journal of Transpersonal Psychology* 16, no. 1 (1984): 63–73.

_____. *Toward a Psychology of Awakening: Buddhism, Psychotherapy, and the Path of Personal and Spiritual Transformation.* Boston: Shambhala, 2000, 2002.

Whitfield, Charles L. Foreword to *Spiritual Awakenings: Insights of the Near-Death Experience and Other Doorways to Our Soul* by Barbara Harris Whitfield. Deerfield Beach, FL: Health Communications, 1995.

_____. *Alcoholism, Attachments and Spirituality: A Transpersonal Approach.* East Rutherford, NJ: Thomas W. Perrin, 1985.

Wilber, Ken. "The Pre/Trans Fallacy." *Journal of Humanistic Psychology* 22, no. 2 (1982): 5–43.

_____. "The Pre/Trans Fallacy." In *Paths Beyond Ego: The Transpersonal Vision,* edited by Roger Walsh and Frances Vaughan, 124–29. New York: Jeremy P. Tarcher/Putnam, 1993.

Winnicott, Donald W. *The Maturational Processes and the Facilitating Environment: Studies in the Theory of Emotional Development.* Madison, CT: International Universities Press, 1987.

About the Author

INGRID MATHIEU holds a master's degree in transpersonal psychology and a doctorate in clinical psychology from the Institute of Transpersonal Psychology in Palo Alto, California. As a psychotherapist in Beverly Hills, California, she specializes in treating individuals who are in recovery.